PENGUIN MODERN MASTERS
CLAUDE LÉVI-STRAUSS

Edmund Leach is Provost of King's College, Cambridge,
and University Reader in Anthropology. He is considered
to be the foremost critic and interpreter of Lévi-Strauss
as well as one of Britain's leading social anthropologists.
Mr. Leach is the author of numerous articles and books
and is also widely acclaimed for his 1967 Leith Lectures,
"A Runaway World?"

Frank Kermode, King Edward VII Professor of English
Literature at Cambridge, is the author of *The Classic;
D. H. Lawrence; Shakespeare, Spenser, Donne;* and other
widely acclaimed critical studies.

# MODERN MASTERS

PENGUIN
MODERN MASTERS

EDITED BY frank kermode

*By Modern Masters we mean the men who have changed and are changing the life and thought of our age. The authors of these volumes are themselves masters, and they have written their books in the belief that general discussion of their subjects will henceforth be more informed and more exciting than ever before.* —F.K.

# claude
# lévi-strauss

*Revised Edition*

## edmund leach

PENGUIN BOOKS

Penguin Books Ltd, Harmondsworth, Middlesex, England
Penguin Books, 625 Madison Avenue, New York, New York 10022, U.S.A.
Penguin Books Australia Ltd, Ringwood, Victoria, Australia
Penguin Books Canada Ltd, 41 Steelcase Road West, Markham, Ontario, Canada
Penguin Books (N.Z.) Ltd, 182–190 Wairau Road, Auckland 10, New Zealand

First published in Great Britain by Fontana 1970
First published in the United States by The Viking Press 1970
Reprinted 1971 (twice), 1973, 1974
Revised edition published 1974
Reprinted 1975
Published in Penguin Books 1976

ISBN 0 14 00.4300 4

Library of Congress catalog card number: 74-1122

Printed in the United States of America by
Offset Paperback Mfrs., Inc., Dallas, Pennsylvania
Set in Linotype Primer

*Acknowledgment is made to the following for permission to quote
material:*

HILL AND WANG, INC., and JONATHAN CAPE LTD.: From *The Elements of
Seminology* by Roland Barthes. Translated by Dr. Annette Lavers and
Dr. Colin Smith. Translation © Jonathan Cape Ltd., 1967. Reprinted by
permission.

THE UNIVERSITY OF CHICAGO PRESS and GEORGE WEIDENFELD & NICOLSON
LTD.: From *The Savage Mind* by Claude Lévi-Strauss. English translation
© George Weidenfeld & Nicolson Ltd., 1966. All rights reserved. Re-
printed by permission.

# CONTENTS

# BIOGRAPHICAL NOTE

| | |
|---|---|
| 1908 | Born in Belgium. |
| 1914–1918 | Lived with his parents in a house near Versailles. (His father was an artist.) |
| 1927–1932 | Student at the University of Paris, where he took a degree in Law with the *Agrégation de philosophie*. His course of study included reading from works "by the masters of the French School of Sociology"—presumably Saint Simon, Comte, Durkheim, and Mauss. |
| 1932–1934 | Worked as a teacher in a *lycée*. |
| 1934 | Through the patronage of Celestin Bouglé, Director of the Ecole Normale Supérieure, was offered a post as Professor of Sociology at the University of São Paulo, Brazil. (The University had been founded by French initiative, and the French diplomatic mission was still concerned with the recruitment of staff.) |
| 1934–1937 | Professor of Sociology, University of São Paulo. During this period he seems to have returned to France on several occasions. He also made |

brief visits to the interior of Brazil to engage in ethnographic investigations, but by the end of the period he had had about five months of actual field experience.

1934     Read Lowie's *Primitive Society* (1920) in English which was Lévi-Strauss' first introduction to specialist anthropological writing. (E. Métraux's French translation of Lowie's book was not published until 1935.)

1936     First anthropological publication: a forty-five page article on the social organization of the Bororo Indians.

1938–1939     Having resigned from the service of the University of São Paulo he obtained French government financial support for a more extensive expedition to central Brazil. The details of the expedition are hard to determine. Lévi-Strauss initially had two scientific companions engaged in different kinds of research. The party left its base at Cuiaba in June 1938 and reached the junction of the Madeira and Machado rivers by the end of the year. They seem to have been on the move nearly the whole time. Everything that Lévi-Strauss has written about the Nambikwara and Tupi-Kawahib Indians seems to be based on this experience.

1939–1940     In France on military service.

1941     (Spring.) Made his way via Martinique and Puerto Rico to New York to take up a post at the New School for Social Research arranged for him by Robert Lowie, E. Métraux, and Max Ascoli.

1945     Contributed article, "L'analyse structurale en linguistique et en anthropologie," to *Word: Journal of the Linguistic Circle of New York* (founded by Roman Jakobson and his associates).

| | |
|---|---|
| 1946–1947 | French cultural attaché in the United States. |
| 1948 | Publication of *La Vie familiale et sociale des Indiens Nambikwara*. |
| 1949 | Publication of *Les Structures élémentaires de la parenté*. |
| 1950 | Director of Studies at the Ecole pratique des hautes études, University of Paris (Laboratory of Social Anthropology). |
| 1950 | Short field-work trip to Chittagong, East Pakistan. |
| 1952 | Publication of *Race et Histoire*. |
| 1953–1960 | Secretary General of the International Council of the Social Sciences. |
| 1955 | Publication of "The Structural Study of Myth," *Journal of American Folklore*, Vol. 68, No. 270, pp. 428–44, and *Tristes Tropiques*. |
| 1958 | Publication of *Anthropologie structurale*. |
| 1959 | Appointed to Chair of Social Anthropology at the Collège de France. |
| 1960 | Publication of "La Geste d'Asdiwal," in *Annuaire de l'E.P.H.E.*, 5me section, *Sciences Religieuses*, 1958–1959. |
| 1962 | Publication of *Le Totémisme aujourd'hui* and *La Pensée sauvage*. |
| 1964 | Publication of *Mythologiques*, Vol. I: *Le cru et le cuit*. Officer of the Legion of Honor. |
| 1967 | Publication of *Mythologiques*, Vol. II: *Du miel aux cendres*. |
| 1968 | Publication of *Mythologiques*, Vol. III: *L'origine des manières de table*. |
| 1968 | Awarded the Gold Medal of the Centre National de la Recherche Scientifique, "the highest French scientific distinction." |
| 1971 | Publication of *Mythologiques*, Vol. IV: *L'Homme nu*. Commander, National Order of Merit. |
| 1973 | Member of the French Academy. Publication of *Anthropologie structurale deux*. |

CLAUDE LÉVI-STRAUSS

## The Man Himself

# i

Claude Lévi-Strauss, Professor of Social Anthropology at the Collège de France, is, by common consent, the most distinguished exponent of this particular academic trade to be found anywhere outside the English-speaking world, but scholars who call themselves social anthropologists are of two kinds. The prototype of the first was Sir James Frazer (1854–1941), author of *The Golden Bough*. He was a man of monumental learning who had no first-hand acquaintance with the lives of the primitive peoples about whom he wrote. He hoped to discover fundamental truths about the nature of human psychology by comparing the details of human culture on a world-wide scale. The prototype of the second was Bronislaw Malinowski (1884–1942), born in Poland but naturalized an Englishman, who spent most of his academic life analyzing the results of research which he himself had personally conducted over a period of four years in a single small village in far off Melanesia. His aim was to show how this exotic community "functioned" as a social system and how its individual members passed through their lives from the cradle to the grave. He was more interested in the differences between human cultures than in their over-all similarity.

Most of those who at present call themselves social anthropologists in either Britain or the United States claim to be "functionalists"; broadly speaking they are anthropologists in the style and tradition of Malinowski. In contrast, Claude Lévi-Strauss is a social anthropologist in the tradition though not in the style of Frazer. His ultimate concern is to establish facts which are true about "the human mind" rather than about the organization of any particular society or class of societies. The difference is fundamental.

In his day Malinowski had three kinds of celebrity. His renown among the general public was as a prophet of free love. Though tame by modern standards, his accounts of the sexual eccentricities of Trobriand Islanders were rated as near pornography. The almost passionate enthusiasm of professional colleagues rested on other grounds—first, the novelty of his methods of field research, which have now been universally imitated; second, the dogmas of his special brand of "functionalism," an oversimplified, mechanistic style of sociological theorizing now generally viewed with some contempt.

Lévi-Strauss' record has been quite different. From the very start he has been a straight scholar-intellectual. Apart from some engaging photographs of naked Amazonian ladies tucked in at the end of *Tristes Tropiques* (1955), he has refrained from popularizing gimmicks of the kind which led Malinowski to entitle one of his Trobriand monographs *The Sexual Life of Savages*. By Malinowski standards Lévi-Strauss' field research is of only moderate quality. The outstanding characteristic of his writing, whether in French or in English, is that it is difficult to understand; his sociological theories combine baffling complexity with overwhelming erudition. Some readers even suspect that they are being treated to a confidence trick. Even now, despite his immense prestige, the critics among his professional colleagues still greatly outnumber the disciples. Yet his academic importance is unquestioned. Lévi-Strauss is admired not so much for the novelty of his ideas as for the bold originality with which he seeks to apply them. He has suggested new ways of looking at familiar facts; it is the method that is interesting rather than the practical consequences of the use to which it has been put.

The method, as such, is as much linguistic as anthropological, and it has aroused excitement among many different brands of intellectual—students of literature, of politics, of ancient philosophy, of theology, of art. The purpose of this book is to give some indication of why this should be so. But first I must declare a personal prejudice.

I myself was once a pupil of Malinowski, and I am, at heart, still a "functionalist" even though I recognize the limitations of Malinowski's own brand of theory. Although I have occasionally used the "structuralist" methods of Lévi-Strauss to illuminate particular features of particular cultural systems, the gap between my general position and that of Lévi-Strauss is very wide. This difference of viewpoint is bound to show through in the pages which follow. My main task is to give an account of Lévi-Strauss' methods and opinions rather than to offer private comments, but I cannot pretend to be a disinterested observer.

My concern is with Lévi-Strauss' ideas, not his life history, but since his bibliography, starting in 1936, already includes twelve books and well over a hundred substantial articles I have a formidable task. No one could survey such a landscape without introducing distortions and I am going to make matters even worse by ignoring the chronology. I shall start in the middle and work both forward and backward. There is a personal justification for this eccentricity which needs to be explained.

We may think of Lévi-Strauss' writings as a three-pointed star radiating around the autobiographical ethnographic travel book *Tristes Tropiques*. The three limbs of the star would then be labeled (1) kinship theory, (2) the logic of myth, (3) the theory of primitive classification. In my biased estimation the first of these, which is also the earliest, is the least important. This is a value judgment which our author himself does not share. In his later writings Lévi-Strauss frequently refers to *Les Structures élémentaires de la parenté* (1949) as if it were an authoritative landmark in the history of social anthropology, and the substantially revised English-language (1969) edition includes a vigorous polemical counterattack against the views of those English admirers like myself who have dared to suggest that parts of his theory do not fit the facts.

Obviously a book of this sort cannot provide me with a base from which to develop a sympathetic commentary on Lévi-Strauss' general attitude. So I shall leave it until the end. Meanwhile, we need a chronological guide-line, which is to be found on pages ix–xi. Sources are various; down to 1941 most of the information comes from *Tristes Tropiques*, where the dating of events is often rather vague but I am indebted to Professor Lévi-Strauss himself for some minor corrections to the details given in the first English edition of this book.

One further biographical fact which seeps through into a number of Lévi-Strauss' writings, notably in the Introduction (*"ouverture"*) and intricately arranged chapter headings of *Mythologiques I*, is that he is a gifted musician. Lévi-Strauss also recalls that from a very early age he had been intensely interested in geology and that in late adolescence he developed an interest, first in psychoanalysis, and then in Marxism. In *Tristes Tropiques* Lévi-Strauss describes these topics as his "three mistresses," making it quite clear that geology was his first love.

I will come back to the geology in a moment, but first let us glance at his Marxism. Lévi-Strauss himself remarks:

Marxism seemed to me to proceed in the same way as geology and psychoanalysis. . . . All three showed that understanding consists in the reduction of one type of reality to another; that true reality is never the most obvious of realities. . . . In all these cases the problem is the same: the relation . . . between reason and sense-perception. . . . (*Tristes Tropiques* [in English translation], p. 61)[1]

In practice, the relevance of Marxist ideology for an understanding of Lévi-Strauss is difficult to determine. Lévi-Strauss' use of dialectic, with the formal sequence of thesis-antithesis-synthesis, is Hegelian rather than

---

[1] All quotations from *Tristes Tropiques* are taken from the translation by John Russell (New York, 1961).

Marxist, and his attitude to history seems to be quite contrary to Marxist dogma. But the picture is greatly confused by the dialectical interplay between the Existentialism of Sartre and the Structuralism of Lévi-Strauss.

As students in the early thirties Sartre, Lévi-Strauss, Merleau-Ponty, and Simone de Beauvoir were all contemporaries and around 1932 the last three were all together as student teachers in the same *lycée*, but Sartre and Lévi-Strauss only met for the first time in New York. Articles by Lévi-Strauss have frequently appeared in Sartre's journal *Les Temps Modernes* as late as 1961, but by 1955 personal relations between the two men were clearly becoming rather strained. In *Tristes Tropiques* Lévi-Strauss remarks of Existentialism that "to promote private preoccupations to the rank of philosophical problems is dangerous and may end in a kind of shop-girl's philosophy" (*Tristes Tropiques* [in English translation], p. 62), and the whole of Chapter 9 of *La Pensée sauvage* (1962) is devoted to a polemical attack against Sartre's *Critique de la raison dialectique*. Lévi-Strauss is especially scornful of Sartre's (apparent) opinion that the members of exotic societies must necessarily be incapable of intellectual analysis and powers of rational demonstration. Nevertheless he has to admit that "he feels himself very close to Sartre whenever the latter applies himself with incomparable artistry, to grasping, in its dialectical movement, a present or past social experience within our own culture." (*The Savage Mind* [The English translation of *La Pensée sauvage*], p. 250)

But then Sartre is a Marxist; and so also, from time to time, is Lévi-Strauss—or so he says! Both authors freely bespatter their pages with Marxist terminology and denounce the other's misuse of the sacred jargon.

On this matter I can do no more than draw the reader's attention to a commentary by Jean Pouillon (1965) which is strongly reminiscent of Lewis Carroll's account of the non-battle between Tweedledum and Tweedledee.[2]

I am not trying to suggest that Lévi-Strauss' present position is at all close to that of the existentialists; on the contrary it is, in many respects very remote. But Existentialism and Lévi-Strauss' brand of Structuralism have common Marxist roots and the distinction between the two is by no means as sharp as some would like to believe.[3] Despite the savage attack on Sartre, *La Pensée sauvage* is dedicated to the memory of Maurice Merleau-Ponty, the phenomenologist philosopher, whose position was, on the face of it, very much closer to Existentialism than to Structuralism.

The squabble with Sartre over "history" is very similar to Lévi-Strauss' squabble with Paul Ricoeur over "hermeneutic."[4] It stems from a different evaluation of the "arrow of time." For the phenomenologists and the existentialists, history provides the myth which justifies the present, but the present is also a necessary culmination of where history has brought us to. The structuralist position is much less egocentric: history offers us images of past societies which were structural transformations of those we now know, neither better nor worse. We, in our vantage point of the present, are not in a privileged position of superiority. But Lévi-Strauss' own attitude to history is elusive, and I can only advise the persistent inquirer to consult for him-

[2] Jean Pouillon, "Sartre et Lévi-Strauss," *L'Arc* (Aix-en-Provence), No. 26 (1965), pp. 55–60.
[3] Jean Piaget, in *Structuralism* (New York, 1970), adopts definitions that imply that Sartre is a more authentic "structuralist" than is Lévi-Strauss!
[4] Paul Ricoeur, "Structure et herméneutique," *Esprit* (Paris), November 1963, pp. 596–627.

self the densely argued pages 256–64 of *The Savage Mind*.

Two features in Lévi-Strauss' position seem crucial. First, he holds that the study of history diachronically and the study of anthropology cross-culturally but synchronically are two alternative ways of doing the same kind of thing:

> The anthropologist respects history, but he does not accord it a special value. He conceives it as a study complementary to his own; one of them unfurls the range of human societies in time, the other in space. And the difference is even less great than it might seem, since the historian strives to reconstruct the picture of vanished societies as they were at the points which for them corresponded to the present, while the ethnographer does his best to reconstruct the historical stages which temporally preceded their existing form. (*The Savage Mind*, p. 256)

Second, Lévi-Strauss insists that when history takes the form of a recollection of past events it is part of the thinker's present, not of his past. For the thinking human being all recollected experience is contemporaneous; as in myth, all events are part of a single synchronous totality. Here the off-stage model is Proust, and the penultimate chapter of *La Pensée sauvage*, which is entitled "*Le Temps retrouvé*," is plainly intended to echo the final volume of *A la Recherche du temps perdu*, which has the same title.

Incidentally the whole corpus of Lévi-Strauss' writings is packed with oblique references and puns of this kind which recall Verlaine's Symbolist formula "*pas de couleur, rien que la nuance*" ("no color, nothing but nuance"). Davy has remarked that the Symbolist poets "insisted that the function of poetic language and particularly of images was not to illustrate ideas but to embody an otherwise indefinable experience."[5] Readers who find the precise meaning of Lévi-Strauss' prose persistently elusive should remember this part of his literary background.[6]

But on this matter of the structuralist view of history one further point deserves note. Although Lévi-Strauss constantly reaffirms his view that the structures of primitive thought are present in our modern minds just as much as they are in the minds of those who belong to "societies without history," he has been very cautious about trying to demonstrate this equivalence. In *La Pensée sauvage*, as we shall see, he does occasionally consider the application of structuralist arguments to features of the culture of contemporary western Europe, but for the most part he draws a sharp (though arbitrary) line between primitive societies, which are grist for the anthropologist because they are timeless and static, and advanced societies, which elude anthropological analysis because they are "in history." Lévi-Strauss has consistently refused to apply structuralist techniques to the analysis of diachronic sequences. Events in the historical past survive in our consciousness only as myth, and it is an intrinsic characteristic of myth (and also of Lévi-Strauss' structural analysis) that the chronological sequence of events is irrelevant.[7]

It is in this context that Lévi-Strauss' comments on geology become particularly revealing.

[5] Charles B. Davy, *Words in the Mind* (Cambridge, Mass., 1965), p. 54.
[6] This point has been developed at length by James A. Boon, *From Symbolism to Structuralism* (New York, 1972).
[7] For further discussion see, in particular, the contributions by Ricoeur and Lévi-Strauss to the symposium debate "La Pensée sauvage et le structuralisme," *Esprit* (Paris), November 1963.

The presuppositions of nineteenth-century anthropologists were proto-historical—evolutionist or diffusionist, as the case might be. But Lévi-Strauss' time sense is geological. Although, like Tylor and Frazer, he seems to be interested in the customs of contemporary primitive peoples only because he thinks of them as being in some sense primeval, he does not argue, as Frazer might have done that what is primeval is inferior. In a landscape, rocks of immense antiquity may be found alongside sediments of relatively recent origin, but we do not argue on that account that one is inferior to the other. So also with living things (and by implication human societies):

> Sometimes . . . on one side and the other of a hidden crevice we find two green plants of different species. Each has chosen the soil which suits it: and we realize that within the rock are two ammonites, one of which has involutions less complex than the other's. We glimpse, that is to say, a difference of many thousands of years; time and space suddenly commingle; the living diversity of that moment juxtaposes one age and the other and perpetuates them. (*Tristes Tropiques*, p. 60)

Note that it is not really the green plants that arouse Lévi-Strauss' interest; they merely trigger off his curiosity. His deeper concern is with what is underneath—something altogether more abstract: the relationship between two ammonites, residues of living species which ceased to exist millions of years in the past. And yet again the reason he feels justified in being interested in this abstraction is that it throws light on the present—the difference between his two green plants: "Unlike the history of the historians history as the geologist and the psychoanalyst sees it is intended to body forth in time—rather in the manner of a *tableau vivant*—certain fundamental properties of the physical and psychical universe." (*Tristes Tropiques*, pp. 60–61)

This search for "fundamental properties" is a recurrent theme in all Lévi-Strauss' writings, but it is not just a matter of antiquarian curiosity. The point is rather that what is fundamental and universal must be the essence of our true nature, and we can use an understanding of that nature to improve ourselves:

> The second phase of our undertaking is that while not clinging to elements from any one particular society, we make use of all of them in order to distinguish those principles of social life which may be applied to reform our own customs and not those of customs foreign to our own. . . . Our own society is the only one which we can transform and yet not destroy, since the changes which we should introduce would come from within. (*Tristes Tropiques*, pp. 391–92)

As this passage shows, Lévi-Strauss is a visionary, and the trouble with those who see visions is that they find it very difficult to recognize the plain matter-of-fact world which the rest of us see all around. Lévi-Strauss pursues his anthropology because he conceives of primitive peoples as "reduced models" of what is essential in all mankind, but the resulting Rousseau-like noble savages inhabit a world very far removed from the dirt and squalor that are the field anthropologist's normal stamping ground.

This is important. A careful study of *Tristes Tropiques*

reveals that, in the whole course of his Brazilian travels, Lévi-Strauss can never have stayed in one place for more than a few weeks at a time and that he was never able to converse easily with any of his native informants in their native language.

There are many kinds of anthropological inquiry, but Malinowski-style intensive field work employing the vernacular, which is now the standard research technique employed by nearly all British and American social anthropologists, is an entirely different procedure from the careful but uncomprehending description of manners and customs, based on the use of special informants and interpreters, which was the original source for most of the ethnographic observations on which Lévi-Strauss, like his Frazerian predecessors, has chosen to rely.

It is perfectly true that an experienced anthropologist, visiting a "new" primitive society for the first time and working with the aid of competent interpreters, may be able, after a stay of only a few days, to develop in his own mind a fairly comprehensive "model" of how the social system works, but it is also true that if he stays for six months and learns to speak the local language very little of that original "model" will remain. Indeed, the task of understanding how the system works will by then appear even more formidable than it did just two days after his first arrival.

Lévi-Strauss himself has never had the opportunity to suffer this demoralizing experience, and he never comes to grips with the issues involved.

In all his writings Lévi-Strauss assumes that the simple, first-stage "model" generated by the observer's first impressions corresponds quite closely to a genuine (and very important) ethnographic reality—the "conscious model" which is present in the minds of the anthropologist's informants. In contrast, to anthropologists who have had a wider and more varied range of field experience, it seems all too obvious that this initial model is little more than an amalgam of the observer's own prejudiced presuppositions.

On this account many would argue that Lévi-Strauss, like Frazer, is insufficiently critical of his source material. He always seems to be able to find just what he is looking for. Any evidence, however dubious, is acceptable so long as it fits with logically calculated expectations; but wherever the data run counter to the theory Lévi-Strauss will either bypass the evidence or marshal the full resources of his powerful invective to have the heresy thrown out of court. So we need to remember that Lévi-Strauss' prime training was in philosophy and law; he consistently behaves like an advocate defending a cause rather than a scientist searching for ultimate truth.

But the philosopher-advocate is also a poet. William Empson's *Seven Types of Ambiguity* (1931) belongs to a class of literary criticism which is wholly antipathetic to contemporary structuralists, but none the less it makes excellent introductory reading for any would-be student of Lévi-Strauss. Lévi-Strauss has not actually published poetry, but his whole attitude to the sounds and meanings and combinations and permutations of language elements betrays his nature. His grand four-volume study of the structure of American Indian mythology is not entitled *Mythologies* but *Mythologiques*—the "logics of myth"—and the object of the exercise is to explore the mysterious interconnections between these myth-logics and other logics. This is poet's country, and those who get impatient with the tortuous gymnastics of Lévi-Straussian argument—as most of us do—need to remember that he shares with Freud a most remarkable capacity for leading us all unawares into the innermost recesses of our secret emotions.

## Oysters, Smoked Salmon, and Stilton Cheese

# ii

Lévi-Strauss is distinguished among the intellectuals of his own country as the leading exponent of "Structuralism," a word which has come to be used as if it denoted a whole new philosophy of life on the analogy of "Marxism" or "Existentialism." What is this "Structuralism" all about?

The general argument runs something like this. What we know about the external world we apprehend through our senses. The phenomena we perceive have the characteristics we attribute to them because of the way our senses operate and the way the human brain is designed to order and interpret the stimuli which are fed into it. One very important feature of this ordering process is that we cut up the continua of space and time with which we are surrounded into segments, so that we are predisposed to think of the environment as consisting of vast numbers of separate things belonging to named classes, and to think of the passage of time as consisting of sequences of separate events. Correspondingly, when, as men, we construct artificial things (artifacts of all kinds), or devise ceremonials, or write histories of the past, we imitate our apprehension of nature: the products of our culture are segmented and ordered in the same way as we suppose the products of nature to be segmented and ordered.

Let me give a very simple example of what I mean. The color spectrum, which runs from violet, through blue, to green, to yellow, to red, is a continuum. There is no natural point at which green changes to yellow or yellow to red. Our mental recognition of color is a response to variations in the quality of the light input, notably to luminosity as between dark and light and to wave length as between long and short. Wave length gets shorter as we move from infrared to ultraviolet, while temperature, as measured on a thermometer, gets less; luminosity is zero at either end of this spectrum and reaches a maximum in the middle—that is, in the yellow.[1] It is a discrimination of the human brain which breaks up this continuum into segments so, that we feel that blue, green, yellow, red, etc., are quite "different" colors. This ordering mechanism of the brain is such

---

[1] Physicists must forgive the archaic account of the relation between color and thermal radiation. The practical description of color difference is highly technical but, as an example, the "reflectances" (luminosities) of the three standard artists colors Emerald Green, Chrome Yellow, and Cadmium Red, with wave lengths respectively 512, 581, and 600 millimicrons, are in the ratio 2:3:1: A thermometer placed in different parts of a spectrum derived from a white light source will register the greatest temperature rise in the infrared and the least in the ultraviolet.

that anyone who is not color blind can readily be taught to feel that green is the "opposite" of red in the same way that black is the opposite of white. In our own culture we have in fact been taught to make this discrimination, and because of this we find it appropriate to use red and green signals as if they corresponded to plus and minus. Actually we make a number of oppositions of this kind in which red is contrasted not only with green but also with other "colors," notably white, black, blue, and yellow. When we make paired oppositions of this kind, red is consistently given the same value; it is treated as a danger sign—hot taps, live electric wires, debit entries in account books, stop signs on roads and railways. This is a pattern which turns up in many other cultures besides our own and in these other cases there is often a quite explicit recognition that the "danger" of red derives from its "natural" association with blood.

Anyway, in our case, with traffic lights on both railways and roads, green means go and red means stop. For many situations this is sufficient. However, if we want to devise a further signal with an intermediate meaning—*about to stop / about to go*—we choose the color yellow. We do this because, in the spectrum, it lies midway between green and red.

In this example the ordering of the colors green-yellow-red is the same as the ordering of the instructions *go-caution-stop*; the color system and the signal system have the same "structure," the one is a transformation of the other.

But notice how we have arrived at this transformation:

a) The color spectrum exists in nature as a continuum.

b) The human brain interprets this continuum as if it consisted of discontinuous segments.

c) The human brain searches for an appropriate representation of a binary opposition plus/minus and selects green and red as a binary pair.

d) Having set up this polar opposition, the human brain is dissatisfied with the resulting discontinuity and searches for an intermediate position: not plus/not minus.

e) It then goes back to the original natural continuum and chooses yellow as the intermediate signal because the brain is able to perceive yellow as a discontinuous intermediate segment lying between green and red.

f) Thus the final cultural product—the three-color traffic signal—is a simplified imitation of a phenomenon of nature—the color spectrum—as apprehended by the human brain.

The essence of this whole argument may be exhibited in a diagram (Figure 1) which represents two superimposed triangles. The corners of the first triangle are the colors green, yellow, red, which are differentiated along two axes: (1) short wave length/long wave length and (2) low luminosity/high luminosity. The corners of the second triangle are three instructions concerning movement: *go*—continue in a state of movement; *caution*—prepare to change your state of movement; *stop*—continue in a state of non-movement. These messages are again differentiated along two axes: (1) movement/no movement and (2) change/no change. By superimposing one schema on the other the colors become signals for the underlying instructions: the natural structure of the color relations is the same as the logical structure relating the three instructions.

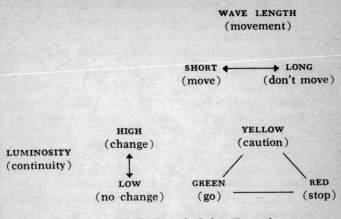

*Figure 1. Traffic-Signal Color Triangle*

This particular example has not, so far as I am aware, ever been used by Lévi-Strauss, but the structuralist thesis is that triangles of this kind, implying comparable transformations of models of nature as apprehended by human brains, have very general application, though in the general case the possibilities are more complicated.

In my example, the pattern was subject to two special constraints: first, it is a "fact of nature" that the sequence of colors in the spectrum is green-yellow-red and not yellow-green-red or green-red-yellow, and second, there is the further fact of nature, which certainly goes back to very early paleolithic times, that human beings have a tendency to make a direct association between *red* as a color and *blood* as a substance, so that, if any one of these three colors is to be selected to mean "stop-danger," it is much more likely to be *red* than either *yellow* or *green*. On this account the correlation between the members of the two triads are, in this case, more or less predetermined. The equivalences $\begin{Bmatrix} \text{red-yellow-green} \\ \text{STOP-CAUTION-GO} \end{Bmatrix}$ are given and we do not need to pay attention to alternative possibilities offered by the rest of the matrix.

| STOP | CAUTION | GO | |
|------|---------|-----|---|
| *red* | *yellow* | *green* | —actual sequence |
| red | green | yellow | |
| yellow | red | green | other |
| yellow | green | red | possible |
| green | yellow | red | sequences |
| green | red | yellow | |

But in the general case, a structural analysis needs to start by setting out *all* the possible permutations and to proceed by examination of the empirical evidence on a comparative basis. Lévi-Strauss himself puts it this way:

The method we adopt . . . consists of the following operations:—
(i) define the phenomenon under study as a relation between two or more terms, real or supposed;
(ii) construct a table of possible permutations between these terms:
(iii) take this table as the general object of analysis which, at this level only, can yield necessary connections, the empirical phenomenon considered at the beginning being only one possible combination among others, the complete system of which must be constructed beforehand. (*Totemism* [English translation of *Le Totémisme aujourd'hui*], p. 16)

As I have explained for the traffic-signal case, the ultimate object of the exercise is to discover how relations which exist in nature (and are apprehended as such by human brains) are used to generate cultural products which incorporate these same relations. This point must not be misunderstood. Lévi-Strauss is not an idealist in the style of Bishop Berkeley; he is not arguing that Nature has no existence other than in its apprehension by human minds. Lévi-Strauss' Nature is a genuine reality "out there"; it is governed by natural laws which are accessible, at least in part, to human scientific investigation, but our capacity to apprehend the nature of Nature is severely restricted by the nature of the apparatus through which we do the apprehending. Lévi-Strauss' thesis is that by noticing *how* we apprehend nature, by observing the qualities of the classifications which we use and the way we manipulate the resulting categories, we shall be able to infer crucial facts about the mechanism of thinking.

After all, since human brains are themselves natural objects and since they are substantially the same throughout the species *Homo sapiens*, we must suppose that when cultural products are generated in the way I have described the process must impart to them certain universal (natural) characteristics of the brain itself. Thus, in investigating the elementary structures of cultural phenomena, we are also making discoveries about the nature of man—facts which are true of you and me as well as of the naked savages of Central Brazil. Lévi-Strauss puts it this way: "Anthropology affords me an intellectual satisfaction: it rejoins at one extreme the history of the world and at the other the history of myself, and it unveils the shared motivation of one and the other at the same moment." (*Tristes Tropiques*, p. 62)

It is important to understand just what is being proposed. In a superficial sense the products of culture are enormously varied, and when an anthropologist sets out to compare, let us say, the culture of the Australian Aborigines with that of the Eskimos or that of the English he is first of all impressed by the differences. Yet since all cultures are the product of human brains, there must be, somewhere beneath the surface, features that are common to all.

This, in itself, is no new idea. A much older generation of anthropologists, notably Adolf Bastian (1826–1905) in Germany and Frazer in England held that because all men belong to one species there must be psychological universals (*Elementargedanken*) which should manifest themselves in the occurrence of similar customs among peoples "who had reached the same stage of evolutionary development" all over the world. Frazer and his contemporaries assiduously compiled immense catalogues of "similar" customs which were designed to exhibit this evolutionary principle. This is *not* what the structuralists are up to. The recurrence of a detail of custom in two different parts of the map is not a matter to which Lévi-Strauss attaches any particular importance. In his view, the universals of human culture exist only at the level of structure, never at the level of manifest fact. We may usefully compare the patterning of the relations which links together sets of human behaviors, but we shall *not* learn anything if we simply compare single cultural items as isolates. In the traffic-signal case, it is the contrast between the colors and the switching from one color to another that provides the information; each color has relevance only in relation to the others.

These very general ideas are a development of arguments originally developed by the Prague school of structural linguists but particularly by Roman Jakobson

(1896–      ), who has resided in the United States since 1942 and who was an academic colleague of Lévi-Strauss at the New School for Social Research in New York at the end of World War II. The influence on Lévi-Strauss of Jakobson's style of phonemic analysis, which derives in turn from much earlier work of Saussure, has been very marked. Lévi-Strauss repeatedly makes an assumption that other modes of cultural expression, such as kinship systems and folk taxonomies, are organized like human language. This culture/language analogy has been developed out of Jakobson's distinctive feature theory, but Lévi-Strauss has not exploited the additional insights which might have been derived from Chomsky's thinking about generative grammars. Incidentally, Chomsky himself has expressly declared that Lévi-Strauss' use of linguistic analogies is unjustified, though he agrees that Jakobson's argument must constitute a basic part of any general linguistic theory, including his own.[2, 3]

It is interesting to see how Lévi-Strauss sets about deriving his cultural generalizations from his linguistic

[2] See Noam Chomsky, *Current Issues in Linguistic Theory* (The Hague, 1964), p. 67.

[3] In the view of many professional linguists the publication of Noam Chomsky's *Syntactic Structures* (1957) had a significance for linguistics comparable to that of Einstein's early papers on relativity theory for physics, and it has sometimes been argued, to Lévi-Strauss' discredit, that in relying on a Jakobson-style linguistics, he is following a model that is no longer viable. Two points need to be made on the other side. First, even if Chomsky's work is an advance on that of Jakobson, it does not invalidate the genuine merits of the latter; second, the characteristics of Chomsky's linguistics, which are subsumed under the titles generative and transformational grammars, have many points in common with the generative and transformational rules for myth analysis which Lévi-Strauss developed on

base. His discussion of the "culinary triangle" provides a case in point. This is one of the major themes which persist throughout the four published volumes of *Mythologiques*, but it has also been the subject of an independent article, which I will summarize here.[4]

Lévi-Strauss begins with a brief reference to Jakobson's thesis in the following terms:

> In all the languages of the world the complex systems of oppositions between the phonemes are no more than a multidirectional elaboration of a more simple system which is common to all, namely the contrast between consonant and vowel, which through the working of a double opposition between compact and diffuse, acute and grave, generates on the one hand what we may call the "vocalic triangle":

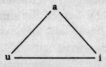

and on the other the "consonant triangle":

---

his own quite independently. But on the other side again, "The idea of a mathematical investigation of language structures, to which Lévi-Strauss occasionally alludes, becomes meaningful only when one considers rules with infinite generative capacity." (Chomsky, p. 66) Lévi-Strauss has been concerned to demonstrate only that varieties of cultural forms, as they are actually recorded, are transformations of one another. Chomsky has tackled the more fundamental problem of seeking to formulate grammatical rules that will discriminate between transformations which make acceptable sense and those which do not. Why can we say: "The cat sat on the mat," but not "The mat sat on the cat"?

4 Claude Lévi-Strauss, "Le Triangle culinaire," *L'Arc* (Aix-en-Provence), No. 26 (1965), pp. 19–29. English version in *New Society* (London), December 22, 1966, pp. 937–40.

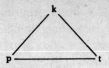

Most readers are likely to find such a pronouncement somewhat baffling, so I will give a rather more extended version of the original doctrine.

Jakobson claims that young children gain control of the basic vowels and consonants so as to generate meaningful noise patterns in a standardized sequence.[5] The child first develops the basic vowel/consonant opposition by discriminating a contrast in loudness:

| Vowel (V) | / | Consonant (C) |
| (high-energy noise) | / | (low-energy noise) |
| (loud-compact) | / | (soft-diffuse) |

The undifferentiated consonant (C) is then split by discriminating pitch—a low-frequency (grave) component ("p") and a high-frequency (acute) component ("t"). The high-energy (compact) velar stop consonant ("k") then complements the undifferentiated high-energy (compact) vowel ("a") while the low-energy (diffuse) consonants ("p," "t") are complemented by corresponding low-energy (diffuse) vowels ("u"-grave, "i"-acute).

The whole argument may be represented by a double triangle of consonants and vowels (Figure 2) discriminated as compact/diffuse, and grave/acute.

But let me go back to the "culinary triangle." After his initial brief reference to the linguistic prototype,

[5] See R. Jakobson and M. Halle, *Fundamentals of Language* (New York, 1956), pp. 38 *ff*.

*Could this explain*
*has values disappear into*
*i in some Eng-diphthongs?*
*(e.g. [aɪt], [maɪt] ~ [mekænɪk]))*

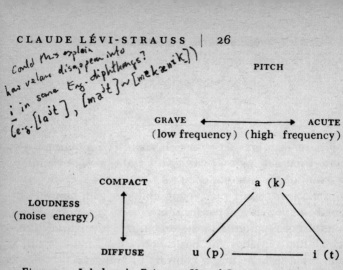

*Figure* 2. *Jakobson's Primary Vowel-Consonant Triangle*

Lévi-Strauss observes that just as there is no human society which lacks a spoken language so also there is no human society which does not, in one way or another, process some of its food supply by cooking. But cooked food may be thought of as fresh raw food which has been transformed (*élaboré*) by cultural means, whereas rotten food is fresh raw food which has been transformed by natural means. Thus, just as Jakobson's vowel-consonant triangles represent the binary oppositions compact/diffuse and grave/acute which have become internalized into the child's computer-like mental processes, so also we can construct a culinary triangle to represent the binary oppositions normal/transformed and culture/nature, which are (by implication) internalized into the *eidos* of human culture everywhere.[6]

[6] For this use of the term *eidos* see Gregory Bateson, *Naven* (New York, 1936), p. 220. In Bateson's language *eidos* refers to "a standardization of the cognitive aspects of the personality of individuals."

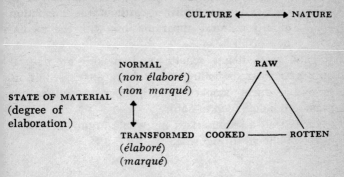

*Figure 3. The Culinary Triangle (Primary Form)*

It is not a necessary part of Lévi-Strauss' argument that raw (unprocessed) food must lie midway between the natural and the cultural, though it is, of course, a fact that most unprocessed human foodstuffs fall into the category "domesticated plants and animals," i.e., they *are* both cultural and natural.

Finally Lévi-Strauss completes his exercise in intellectual gymnastics by claiming that the principal modes of cooking form another structured set which is the converse of the first:

(a) *Roasting* is a process in which the meat is brought into direct contact with the agent of conversion (fire) without the mediation of any cultural apparatus or of air or of water; the process is only partial—roast meat is only partly cooked.

(b) *Boiling* is a process which reduces the raw food to a decomposed state similar to natural rotting, but it requires the mediation of both water and a receptable—an object of culture.

(c) *Smoking* is a process of slow but complete cooking; it is accomplished without the mediation of any cultural apparatus, but with the mediation of air.

Thus, as to means, roasting and smoking are natural processes whereas boiling is a cultural process, but, as to end-products, smoked food belongs to culture but roast and boiled food to nature.

Lévi-Strauss summarizes his whole argument in the diagram shown in Figure 4.

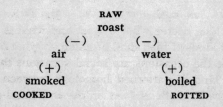

*Figure 4. The Culinary Triangle (Developed Form)*

In his original article, "Le Triangle culinaire," Lévi-Strauss qualifies the generality of this schema by noting that our own system, which distinguishes *grilling* from *roasting*, and *steaming* from *boiling*, and adds a category *frying* (which is a form of boiling in which oil is substituted for water), requires a much more complicated model—and at this point some English-speaking readers might begin to suspect that the whole argument was an elaborate academic joke. But exactly the same diagram (Figure 4) appears on page 406 of *Mythologiques III* (1968) accompanied by the same text, so we must try to take the matter seriously. This is rather difficult. Lévi-Strauss has not adhered to his own rules of procedure as specified above (page 20), and the whole operation suggests a game of acrostics in which appropriate words have been slipped into the vacant slots of a prearranged verbal matrix. Elsewhere Lévi-Strauss has claimed that "behind all sense there is a non-sense"[7] but perhaps the best that one could claim for this fandangle is that behind the nonsense there is a sense, even if it is not the sense of ordinary conversation.

What Lévi-Strauss is getting at is this. *Animals* just eat food, and food is anything which is available which their instincts place in the category "edible." But *human beings*, once they have been weaned from the mother's breast, have no such instincts. It is the conventions of society which decree what is food and what is not food and what kinds of food shall be eaten on what occasions. And since the occasions are social occasions there must be some kind of patterned homology between relationships between kinds of food on the one hand and relationships between social occasions on the other.

Moreover, when we look into the facts, the categories which are treated as significant *kinds* of food become interesting in themselves. The diet of any particular human population is dependent upon the availability of resources and, at the level of actual items of foodstuff (bread, meat, cheese and so on), there is very little overlap between the shopping list of an English housewife and the inventory of comestibles available to an Amazonian Indian. But the English housewife and the Amazonian Indian alike break up the unitary category "food" into a number of subcategories, "food A," "food B," "food C," etc., each of which is treated in a different way. But, at *this* level, the categories A, B,

[7] Claude Lévi-Strauss, "Réponses à quelques questions," *Esprit* (Paris), November 1963, pp. 628–53.

C, etc., turn out to be remarkably alike everywhere. They are, in fact, categories of the kind which appear in Figure 4, and the significant thing about such categories is that they are accorded very different levels of social prestige. I do not mean only that the different components of the feast can always be fitted into our prearranged slots—oysters (raw), smoked salmon (smoked), lobster soup (boiled), saddle of mutton (roast), soufflé (cooked), Stilton cheese (rotted)—but rather that foods of these different general classes bear a standardized relationship to each other. For example, according to our conventions, whenever the menu includes a dish of roast meat it will be accorded pride of place in the middle; steamed and boiled foods, on the other hand, are considered especially suitable for invalids and children. Why should this be? Why should we tend to think of boiled fowl as a homely dish but of roast chicken as a party dish?

All sorts of rationalizations can be devised to fit any particular case—for example that boiling fowls are cheaper than roasters, or that boiled food is "more digestible" (what is the evidence for this?), but all such explanations begin to look rather thin once it is realized that other peoples, with very different cultures from our own, sort out their foodstuffs in very similar ways and apply status distinctions of comparable sort. Some foods are appropriate only to men, others only to women; some foods are forbidden to children; some can only be eaten on ceremonial occasions. The resulting pattern is not always the same, but it is certainly very far from random: Lévi-Strauss has even claimed that the high status which attaches to roasting as against boiling is a *universal* cultural characteristic, so that boiled food is highly regarded only in relatively democratic types of society. "Boiling provides a means of complete conservation of the meat and its juices, whereas roasting is accompanied by destruction and loss. Thus one denotes economy; the other prodigality; the latter is aristocratic, the former plebeian." ("Le Triangle culinaire," p. 23)

An odd line of thought, certainly, yet if we accept Lévi-Strauss' unexpected frame of reference, such comments are not nearly so arbitrary as they may appear. In that we are men, we are all a part of nature; in that we are human beings, we are all a part of culture. Our survival as men depends on our ingestion of food (which is a part of nature); our survival as human beings depends upon our use of social categories which are derived from cultural classifications imposed on elements of nature. The social use of categories of food is thus homologous with the social use of categories of color in the traffic-signal case (page 19). But food is an especially appropriate "mediator" because, when we eat, we do establish, in a literal sense, a direct identity between ourselves (culture) and our food (nature). Cooking is thus universally a means by which nature is transformed into culture, and categories of cooking are always peculiarly appropriate for use as symbols of social differentiation.

In another context, in which Lévi-Strauss is concerned to debunk the anthropological mystique that has clustered around the concept of totemism, he has criticized the functionalist thesis that totemic species are given social value because they are of economic value. On the contrary, says Lévi-Strauss, it is the species themselves considered simply as categories that are socially valuable: totemic species are "goods to think with" (*bonnes à penser*) rather than "goods to eat" (*bonnes à manger*). The culinary triangle is the other side of the same argument. Foodstuffs, as such, are of course "goods to eat"; but this alone does not explain the complications which we inject into the classification of food; food *species*, like totemic *species*, are "goods to think with."[8] (Cf. pages 40–42.)

This is an unfamiliar style of discourse, and it has to be admitted that here, as elsewhere in Lévi-Strauss' writings, there is an element of verbal sleight of hand which invites caution rather than enthusiasm. All the same, the reader should not imagine that the "culinary triangle" is just an elegant *jeu d'esprit* by a master of the unexpected analogy. Lévi-Strauss has by now marshaled a great deal of evidence to show that the processes of food preparation and the categories of food with which they are associated are everywhere elaborately structured and that there are universal principles underlying these structures. Moreover, the method of analysis, however bizarre it may appear, has wide application. The culinary triangle first appeared in print only in 1965, but triangles of comparable type occur in many earlier parts of the Lévi-Straussian corpus.

In the 1945 paper which is the foundation work for all his subsequent structural anthropology. "L'Analyse structurale en linguistique et en anthropologie,"[9] the corners of the triangle are MUTUALITY, RIGHTS, OBLIGATIONS, while the binary oppositions appear to be exchange/no exchange and receivers/givers. In *Les*

---

[8] Several critics have rebuked me for mistranslation, but in fact I cite Lévi-Strauss' own words to avoid this imputation. Literally, *bonnes à penser* means "good to think," *bonnes à manger* "good to eat." But "good to think" is not English, and the adjectival plural of the French is untranslatable. It seems to me that here, as so often, Lévi-Strauss is playing a verbal game. Totemic species are categories of things, and it does in fact convey the meaning better to refer to them as "goods" than my critics would allow.

[9] An English translation of this paper appears as Chapter 2 of *Structural Anthropology* (New York, 1963), the English version of *Anthropologie structurale* (Paris, 1958).

*Structures élémentaires de la parenté* (1949), the triangle becomes BILATERAL MARRIAGE, PATRILATERAL CROSS-COUSIN MARRIAGE, MATRILATERAL CROSS-COUSIN MARRIAGE, and the oppositions are symmetry/asymmetry, alternation/repetition. "La Geste d'Asdiwal" (1960) includes a highly complicated triangle which combines geographical and food category parameters in such a way that vegetable food is opposed to animal food, sea to land, East to West, and definition to lack of definition.[10] This is not just a game. Lévi-Strauss is endeavoring to establish the rudiments of a semantic algebra. If cultural behavior is capable of conveying information then the code in which cultural messages are expressed must have an algebraic structure. It is possible that Lévi-Strauss is making larger claims for the importance of this algebra than is justified by the evidence, but there is more to it than a trickster's game of tic-tac-toe. Let us go back to the beginning.

[10] An English translation, "The Story of Asdiwal," may be found in E. R. Leach, ed., *The Structural Study of Myth and Totemism* (London, 1967), pp. 1–48.

# The Human Animal and His Symbols

● ● ●

# iii

Lévi-Strauss' central intellectual puzzle is one to which European philosophers have returned over and over again; indeed, if we accept Lévi-Strauss' own view of the matter it is a problem which puzzles all mankind, everywhere, always. Quite simply: What is man? Man is an animal, a member of the species *Homo sapiens*, closely related to the great apes and more distantly to all other living species past and present. But man, we assert, is a human being, and in saying that we evidently mean that he is, in some way, other than "just an animal." But in what way is he other? The concept of humanity as distinct from animality does not readily translate into exotic languages, but it is Lévi-Strauss' thesis that a distinction of this sort—corresponding to the opposition culture/nature—is always latent in men's customary attitudes and behaviors

even when it is not explicitly formulated in words. The
human Ego is never by himself; there is no "I" that is
not part of a "We,"[1] and indeed every "I" is a member of
many "We"s. In one sense these we-groups stretch out
to infinity in all directions to embrace everybody and
everything. "Man is not alone in the universe, any more
than the individual is alone in the group, or any one
society alone among other societies" (*Tristes Tropiques*,
p. 398), but in practice we cut up the continua. My
particular "we," the people of *my* family, *my* community, *my* tribe, *my* class—these are altogether special,
they are superior, they are civilized, cultured; the others
are just savages, like wild beasts.

Lévi-Strauss' central preoccupation is to explore the
dialectical process by which this apotheosis of ourselves
as human and godlike and other than animal is formed
and re-formed and bent back upon itself. Adam and
Eve were created as ignorant savages in Paradise in a
world in which animals talked and were helpmeets to
man; it was through sin that they gained knowledge
and became human, and different, and superior to the
animals. But are we really "superior"? God made man
in his own image, but are we so sure that in achieving
humanity (culture) we did not separate ourselves from
God? This is the note on which Lévi-Strauss ends *Tristes
Tropiques*, the book which first brought him interna-
tional renown outside the narrow world of professional
anthropology—to discover the nature of man we must
find our way back to an understanding of how man is
related to nature—and he comes back to the same
theme in the closing paragraph of *Mythologiques III*.
We (Europeans), he comments, have been taught from

[1] *Tristes Tropiques* (Paris, 1955), p. 448: "Le moi n'a pas de
place entre un *nous* et un *rien*."

infancy to be self-centered and individualistic, to fear the impurity of foreign things—a doctrine which we embody in the formula "Hell is the others" (*l'enfer, c'est les autres*)—but primitive myth has the opposite moral implication, "Hell is ourselves" (*l'enfer, c'est nous-même*).[2] "In a century when man is bent on the destruction of innumerable forms of life," it is necessary to insist, as in the myths, "that a properly appointed humanism cannot begin of its own accord but must place the world before life, life before man, and the respect of others before self-interest." (*Mythologiques III*, p. 422) But, the puzzle remains, what is a human being? Where does culture divide off from nature?

Lévi-Strauss himself takes his cue from Rousseau, though he might equally well have followed Vico or Hobbes or Aristotle or a dozen others. It is language which makes man different: "*Qui dit homme, dit langage, et qui dit langage dit société.*" (*Tristes Tropiques*, p. 421) But the emergence of language which accompanies the shift from animality to humanity, from nature to culture, is also a shift from affectivity to a state of reasoning: "The first speech was all in poetry; reasoning was thought of only long afterwards."[3]

Rousseau's thesis, as elaborated by Lévi-Strauss, is that man can become self-conscious—aware of himself as a member of a we-group—only when he becomes capable of employing metaphor as an instrument of contrast and comparison:

---

[2] The reader is expected to recognize that *l'enfer c'est les autres* is a quotation from Jean-Paul Sartre's play *Huis clos* (Paris, 1944).

[3] Jean-Jacques Rousseau, "Essai sur l'origine des langues" (Geneva, 1783).

It is only because man originally felt himself identical to all those like him (among which, as Rousseau explicitly says, we must include animals) that he came to acquire the capacity to distinguish *himself* as he distinguishes *them*, i.e. to use the diversity of species as conceptual support for social differentiation. (*Totemism*, p. 101)

Rousseau's insight can be held to be "true" only in a strictly poetic sense, for the thought processes of proto-man are even less accessible to us than those of apes and monkeys. But the phylogenetic form of the argument is mixed up with Lévi-Strauss' search for human universals. Verbal categories provide the mechanism through which *universal* structural characteristics of human brains are transformed into *universal* structural characteristics of human culture. But if these universals exist, they must, at some rather deep level, be considered innate. In that case, we must suppose that they are patterns which, in the course of human evolution, have become internalized into the human psyche along with the specialized development of those parts of the human brain which are directly concerned with speech formation through the larynx and mouth and with speech reception through the ear. And why not? After all, although the human infant is not born with any innate language, it *is* born with an innate capacity to learn both how to make meaningful utterances and how to decode the meaningful utterances of others.

Not only that but, if Jakobson's argument is correct, all human children will learn to master the basic elements of their phonemic inventory by making the same, or very nearly the same, initial series of basic discriminations—consonant/vowel, nasal consonant/oral stop, grave/acute, compact/diffuse. They presumably do this not so much because of any instinct but because the architecture of the human mouth and throat and its associated musculature makes this the *natural* way to go about it. Lévi-Strauss asks us to believe that category formation in human beings follows similar universal "natural" paths. It is not that it *must* always happen the same way everywhere but that the human brain is so constructed that it is predisposed to develop categories of a particular kind in a particular way.[4]

All animals have a certain limited capacity to make category distinctions. Any mammal or bird can, under appropriate conditions, recognize other members of its own species and distinguish males from females; some can further recognize a category of predator enemies. Human beings, in the process of learning to talk, extend this category-forming capacity to a degree that has no parallel among other creatures, but nevertheless, at its very roots, before the individual's language capacity has become elaborated, category formation must be animal-like rather than human-like. At this basic level the individual (whether animal or human) is concerned only with very simple problems: the distinction between own species and other, dominance and submission, sexual availability or lack of availability, what is edible and what is not. In a natural environment distinctions of this sort are all that are necessary for individual survival, but they are *not* sufficient within a human environment. For human (as distinct from animal) survival every member of society must learn to distinguish

---

[4] It should be stressed, however, that unlike Piaget Lévi-Strauss does not speculate about the ontogenetic or philogenetic development of category systems; he simply relies on this style of argument to explain the otherwise surprising fact that he is able to discover strikingly similar "structures" in widely different cultural contexts.

his fellow men according to their mutual social status.
But the simplest way to do this is to apply transformations of the animal-level categories to the social classification of human beings. This is the key point in
Lévi-Strauss' structuralist approach to the classic anthropological theme of totemism.

It is a fact of empirical observation that human
beings everywhere adopt ritual attitudes toward the
animals and plants in their vicinity. Consider, for example, the separate, and often bizarre, rules which
govern the behavior of Englishmen toward the creatures
which they classify as (1) wild animals, (2) foxes, (3)
game, (4) farm animals, (5) pets, (6) vermin. Notice
further that if we take the sequence of words (1a)
strangers, (2a) enemies, (3a) friends, (4a) neighbors,
(5a) companions, (6a) criminals, the two sets of terms
are in some degree homologous. By a metaphorical
usage the categories of animals could be (and sometimes are) used as equivalents for the categories of
human beings. One of Lévi-Strauss' major contributions
to our understanding has been to show how very widespread is this kind of socialization of animal categories.
The facts themselves are well known, but, in Lévi-
Strauss' view they have been misunderstood.

The conventions by which primitive peoples use
species of plants and animals as symbols for categories
of men are not really any more eccentric than our own,
but,. in a technologically restricted environment, they
become much more noticeable, and to scholars of Sir
James Frazer's generation they seemed altogether extraordinary—so much so that any social equivalence
between human beings and other natural species came
to be regarded as a kind of cult (totemism), a proto-
religion appropriate only to people at a very early stage
of development. It was recognized right from the start

that elements of "totemic" behavior occur even in sophisticated cultures, but the earlier writers interpreted these details as archaic residues which had somehow survived into our own day from the remote past. In the more general primitive case "totemism" was thought to pose a basic problem of rationality.

Why should sane human beings indulge in the "superstitious worship" of animals and plants? How can men come to imagine that they are descended from kangaroos, or wallabies, or white cockatoos? A great variety of possible answers to such questions were proposed. A. Van Gennep, in *L'Etat actuel du problème totémique* (1920), was able to distinguish forty-one different "theories of totemism," and more have accumulated since then. Broadly speaking they fall into two types: (1) universalist explanations implying that totemic beliefs and practices indicate a "childish" mentality which had once been characteristic of all mankind; (2) particularist explanations resting on the functionalist proposition that any totemic system will serve to attach emotional interest to animal and plant species which are of economic value to the particular human society concerned and will thereby tend to preserve these species from total destruction by human depredation.

After the publication of A. Goldenweiser's "Totemism, an Analytical Study" (1910) theories of the first kind were barely tenable, and thereafter down to 1962 the more worth-while contributions to the subject were concerned with particular ethnographies—Australia, Tikopia, Tallensi—rather than with universal truth. But Radcliffe-Brown's "The Sociological Theory of Totemism" (1929) is a special case because it attempts to generalize the functionalist position; "totemism" is here treated as a near universal and is seen as the ritual expression of interdependence between social order and the natural environment. In a later essay, "The Comparative Method in Social Anthropology" (1951), Radcliffe-Brown carried this universalist thesis a good deal further, drawing special attention to the classificatory nature of totemic systems. Some features of this latter paper are so markedly "structuralist" in style that it provided the trigger for Lévi-Strauss' own contribution, *Le Totémisme aujourd'hui* (1962).

Lévi-Strauss takes the view that the anthropologists who have tried to isolate "totemism" as a phenomenon *sui generis* have deluded themselves; considered as a religious system "totemism" is an anthropological mirage; even so, the subject deserves our close attention because totemic beliefs and practices exemplify a universal characteristic of human thought.

Lévi-Strauss' account does not add anything of significance to our understanding of Australian totemism but his reappraisal of Radcliffe-Brown's arguments makes it much easier to understand how the seemingly bizarre thought categories of the Australian Aborigines are related to category systems with which we are more familiar. The crux of his argument is that totemic systems always embody metaphoric systems of the sort indicated above (pages 39–41).[5] Incidentally it was with reference to "totemism" that Lévi-Strauss came up with his own summary of what constitutes the essence of structuralist method, which I have quoted already (see page 20). Note in particular his seeming contempt for the "empirical phenomenon." The "general object of analysis" is conceived as a kind of algebraic matrix of possible permutations and combinations located in the

---

[5] This metaphoric formation is discussed in greater detail below, pages 46–50.

unconscious "human mind"; the empirical evidence is merely an example of what is possible. This same preference for the generalized abstraction as compared with the empirical fact occurs again and again throughout Lévi-Strauss' writings. Mind you, that is not how Lévi-Strauss himself sees the situation. He conceives of the 'human mind" as having objective existence; it is an attribute of human brains. We can ascertain attributes of this human mind by investigating and comparing its cultural products. The study of "empirical phenomena" is thus an essential part of the process of discovery, but it is only a means to an end.[6]

But let us go back to Rousseau's vision of man as a talking animal. Until a few years ago it was customary for anthropologists to draw a very sharp distinction between culture, which was conceived of as exclusively human, and nature, which was common to all animals, including man. This distinction, according to Leslie White, "is one of kind not of degree. And the gap between the two types is of the greatest importance. . . . Man uses symbols; no other creature does. An organism has the ability to symbol or it does not, there are no intermediate stages."[7] In his earlier writings, though less emphatically in his later ones, Lévi-Strauss reiterates this view. The special marker of symbolic thought is the existence of spoken language in which words stand for (signify) things "out there" which are signified.

[6] It is the constant refrain of Lévi-Strauss and his close disciples that all his Anglo-Saxon critics, the present author included, are crude empiricists. Empiricism here seems to mean the doctrine that truth must be verifiable by reference to observable facts; it stands opposed to "rationalism," which reaches to a deeper form of truth by means of operations of the intellect.
[7] Leslie White, *The Science of Culture* (New York, 1949), p. 25.

Signs must be distinguished from triggers. Animals of all kinds respond mechanically to appropriate signals; this process does *not* entail "symbolic thought." In order to be able to operate with symbols it is necessary first of all to be able to distinguish between the sign and the thing it signifies and then to be able to recognize that there is a relation between the sign and the thing signified. This is the cardinal characteristic which distinguishes human thought from animal response— the ability to distinguish A from B while at the same time recognizing that A and B are somehow interdependent.

This distinction can be put in another way. When an individual acts as an individual, operating upon the world outside himself—e.g., if he uses a spade to dig a hole in the ground—he is *not* concerned with symbolization; but the moment some other individual comes onto the scene *every* action, however trivial, serves to communicate information about the actor to the observer—the observed details are interpreted as signs, because observer and actor are in relation. From this point of view the animals in any human environment serve as things with which to think (*bonnes à penser*).

When Lévi-Strauss poses for himself the seemingly quite unanswerable puzzle of how this faculty for symbolic interpretation came into being, he finds his answer in an adaptation of ideas borrowed from Durkheim and his immediate pupils. Certain binary concepts are part of man's nature—e.g., men and women are alike in one sense yet opposite and interdependent in another; the right hand and the left hand are, likewise, equal and opposite, yet related. In society as it actually exists we find that such natural pairs are invariably loaded with cultural significance—they are made into the prototype symbols of the good and the bad, the permitted and the forbidden. Furthermore, in society as it actually exists individuals are social persons who are "in relation" to one another—e.g., as father to son or as employer to employee. These individuals communicate with one another by "exchange"; they exchange words; they exchange gifts. These words and gifts communicate information because they are signs, not because they are things in themselves. When an employer pays out wages to an employee, the action *signifies* the relative status of the parties to the transaction. But, according to Lévi-Strauss (if I understand him correctly), the ultimate basic symbolic exchange which provides the model for all the others is sexual. The incest taboo (which Lévi-Strauss erroneously claims to be "universal") implies a capacity to distinguish between women who are permitted and women who are forbidden and thus generates a distinction between women of the category *wife* and women of the category *sister*. The *basis* of human exchange, and hence the basis of symbolic thought and the beginning of culture, lies in the uniquely human phenomenon that a man is able to establish relationship with another man by means of an exchange of women.[8]

But let me take up once more my earlier point that Lévi-Strauss seems to be more interested in an algebra of possibilities than in the empirical facts. His justification is this: in actual social life individuals communicate with one another all the time by elaborate combinations of signs—by words, by the clothes they wear, by the food they eat, by the way they stand, by the way they arrange the furniture of a room, and so on. In any particular case there will be a certain discoverable consistency between behaviors at these different

[8] I shall come back to this again. See below, Chapter VI, pages 105 *ff.*

levels; e.g., in England, members of the upper middle class living in Kensington will adopt, for each of the "codes" I have mentioned, quite a different style from members of, say, the working class in Leeds. But any particular empirical case is only one alternative from a whole set of possibilities, and, according to Lévi-Strauss and his followers, we shall gain additional insight into the empirical cases that we *have* observed by considering their relationship to the possible cases that we have *not* observed.

At this point it is necessary to make something of a digression. Lévi-Strauss' ideas about how human beings are able to communicate through symbols are a development from arguments originally developed by specialists in structural linguistics and semiology (the theory of signs). But the latter have used a very varied and confusing terminology and it may help if I try to sort out some of the equivalents.

The first basic distinction is that of de Saussure between language (*langue*) and speech (*parole*).[9] "The English language" denotes a total system of words, conventions, and usages; from the point of view of any particular individual speaker it is a "given"; it is not something he creates for himself; the parts of the language are available for use, but they do not have to be used. But when I, as an individual, make an utterance I use "speech"; I select from the total system of "the.language" certain words and grammatical conventions and tones and accents, and by placing these in a particular *order* I am able to transmit information by my utterance.

There is a close but not exact equivalence between the distinction of *language* and *speech*, as specified

[9] F. de Saussure, *Cours de linguistique générale* (Paris, 1916).

above, and the information-theory distinction of *code* and *message*. If we, in fact, think of a spoken language as a code, then it is a particular kind of code—namely, a code made up of sound elements. But there are many other kinds of possible codes. As I suggested just now, we use clothes as a code, or kinds of food, or gestures, or postures, and so on. Each such code is "a language" (in de Saussure's sense), and the sum of all such codes (i.e., the culture of the individual actor) is also "a language."

Now, the verbal boxes which I have used in this argument—e.g., "sound elements," "clothes," "kinds of food," etc.—lump things together because they are associated in our minds as somehow similar in function or "meaning," whereas when I make a verbal utterance and transmit a message—"the cat sat on the mat" —the elements are brought together in a chain as a result of the rules of the language and not because they are in any way similar in themselves. This is what I mean when I refer later to "syntagmatic chains"—they are chains formed by the application of rules of syntax.

In the same way, we need to distinguish the mental association which tells us that roast turkey and boiled chicken are both "kinds of food" (and therefore parts of one language) from the rules of particular whole languages (cultures) which may specify, for example, that in England roast beef should be eaten with Yorkshire pudding or, to be more complex, that a menu of roast turkey followed by flaming plum pudding and mince pies probably indicates that it is December 25.

Many readers are likely to find this use of the word "language" to refer to nonverbal forms of communication somewhat confusing, and matters are not made any easier by the fact that Roland Barthes, who in

*Elements of Semiology* (1968) presents the general structuralist argument with relative clarity, uses yet another terminology. On page 49 I give a modified version of a table which Barthes employs to explain the relationship between metaphoric (paradigmatic) and metonymic (syntagmatic) uses of nonverbal signs. In the original Barthes uses the term "system" in two different senses—first, to denote what I have referred to above as "a language" and, second, to denote the "parts of speech" of such a language—i.e., the sets of objects which correspond to the sets of words which, in a verbal language, we would distinguish as nouns, verbs, adjectives, etc. (I have modified his diagram by writing the first of these usages *"system"* and the second *system*). The term "syntagm," as applied to an assemblage of nonverbal signs, here corresponds to "sentence" in a verbal language.

The distinction between columns A and B in this diagram is very important for any understanding of Lévi-Strauss' writings, but he himself does not use this terminology. Where Barthes opposes "system" and "syntagm," the corresponding contrasts in Lévi-Strauss are "metaphor" and "metonymy" or sometimes "paradigmatic series" and "syntagmatic chain" (see, for example, page 101). Although the jargon is exasperating, the principles are simple. As Jakobson puts it, metaphor (system, paradigm) relies on the recognition of similarity, and metonymy (syntagm) on the recognition of contiguity.[10]

Lévi-Strauss maintains that in the analysis of myth and of primitive thought generally, we need to distinguish between these two poles. For example, if we

[10] R. Jakobson and M. Halle, *Fundamentals of Language* (New York, 1956), p. 81.

Syntagm and System[11]

| A | | B |
|---|---|---|
| System [Parts of speech: nouns, verbs, etc.] | | Syntagm [Sentence.] |
| Garment "system" [language, code] | Set of pieces, parts, or details which cannot be worn at the same time on the same part of the body, and whose variation corresponds to a change in the meaning of the clothing: toque, bonnet, hood, etc. | Juxtaposition in the same type of dress of different elements: skirt, blouse, jacket. |
| Food "system" [language, code] | Set of foodstuffs which have affinities or differences, within which one chooses a dish in view of a certain meaning: entree, roast, sweet, etc.* | Real sequences of dishes chosen during a meal, the menu.* |
| Furniture "system" [language, code] | Set of "stylistic" varieties of a single piece of furniture: bed, etc. | Juxtaposition of different pieces of furniture in the same space: bed, wardrobe, table, etc. |
| Architecture "system" [language code] | Variations in style of a single element in a building: types of roof, balcony, hall, etc. | Sequence of the details at the level of the whole building. |

[11] From Roland Barthes, *Elements of Semiology* (New York, 1968), p. 63. The words in square brackets have been added.

* A restaurant menu actualizes both planes: a horizontal reading of the entrees, for instance, corresponds to the system; a vertical reading of the menu corresponds to the syntagm.

imagine another world peopled by supernatural being;
then we can represent this other world in any number
of ways: as a society of birds, or of fishes, or of wild
animals, or even of beings "like" men, and in each case
we shall be using metaphor. That is one kind of symboli
zation. But there is also another kind in which we rely
on the fact that our audience, being aware of how a
particular syntagm (sentence) is formed out of the
elements of the "system" (language, code), is able to
recognize the whole by being shown only a part. This
is metonymy. For example, when we use the formula
"The Crown stands for Sovereignty" we are relying on
the fact that a crown is uniquely associated with a particular syntagmatic chain of items of clothing which
together form the uniform of a particular officeholder
the King, so that, even when removed from this context of proper use, it can still be used as a signifier for
the whole complex. This metaphor/metonymy opposition is not an either/or distinction; there is always some
element of both kinds of association in any communi-
cative discourse but there can be marked differences of
emphasis. As I have said, "The Crown stands for
Sovereignty" is primarily metonymic; in contrast; the
concept of a "queen bee" is metaphoric.

All this links up with a much earlier style of anthropological analysis. Frazer started his classic study of
primitive magic[12] with the thesis that magical beliefs
depend on two types of (erroneous) mental association:
homeopathic magic, depending on a law of similarity;
and contagious magic, depending on a law of contact.
Frazer's homeopathic/contagious distinction is practi-
cally identical to the Jakobson–Lévi-Strauss meta-

[12] James G. Frazer, *The Golden Bough* (London; abridged edition, 1922), p. 12.

phoric/metonymic distinction, and the fact that Frazer
and Lévi-Strauss should agree that this kind of discrimination is highly relevant for an undersaning of
"primitive thought" seems very significant.

But how does all this tie in with Lévi-Strauss' general
attitude to the process of symbolization?

Well, first of all it needs to be appreciated that
these two dimensions—the metaphoric-paradigmatic-
harmonic-similarity axis on the one hand, and the meto-
nymic-syntagmatic-melodic-contagious axis on the other
—correspond to the logical framework within which
Lévi-Strauss' various structural triangles are constructed.
For example, if we take Figure 3 (page 27), the cul-
ture/nature axis is metaphoric while the normal/trans-
formed axis is metonymic. But it is more immediately
relevant in the present context that, for Lévi-Strauss,
this same framework provides the clue for our understanding of totemism and myth. Considered as individual items of culture totemic rituals or myths are
syntagmatic—they consist of a sequence of details
linked together in a chain; animals and men are apparently interchangeable, culture and nature are confused. But if we take a whole set of such rituals or
myths and superimpose one upon another, then a para-
digmatic-metaphoric pattern emerges; it becomes apparent that the variations of what happens to the
animals are algebraic transformations of the variations
of what happens to the men.

Alternatively we can operate the other way round.
If we start with a particular sequence of customary
behavior we should regard it as a syntagm, a special
case of ordered relations among a set of cultural odd-
ments which, in itself, is just a residue of history. If
we take such a special case and consider the arrangements between its component parts algebraically we can

arrive at the total system, a theme and variations—a set of paradigms (metaphors) of which our special case is just one example. This will bring to our attention all sorts of other possible variations, and we can then take another look at our ethnographic data to see if these other variations actually occur. If they do, then we shall have confirmed that our algebra corresponds to some deep-rooted organizational principle in human brains everywhere.

This sounds plausible in theory, but there are two practical difficulties which turn out to be of major importance. The first is that, in the final stage of this process, it is easy to make it appear that the theory and the evidence fit together, but the contrary is difficult to demonstrate. Logical positivists can therefore argue that Lévi-Strauss' theories are more or less meaningless because, in the last analysis, they cannot be rigorously tested.

The second difficulty is to understand just what is meant by the total system, "the general object of analysis," the ultimate algebraic structure of which particular culture products are merely partial manifestations. Where is this structure located? This is a question which may be asked about all cultural systems. Where is "a spoken language"—in de Saussure's sense—located? The language as a whole is external to any particular individual; in Durkheim's terminology, it is part of the collective consciousness (*conscience collective*) of all those who speak it.

But Lévi-Strauss is not much concerned with the collective consciousness of any particular social system; his quest rather is to discover the collective *unconscious* of "the human mind" (*l'esprit humain*), and this should apply not merely to speakers of one language but to speakers of all languages.

His endeavor sometimes leads him to make statements which suggest that the mind has an autonomy of its own which operates independently of any human individual. For example, "*Nous ne prétendons donc pas montrer comment les hommes pensent dans les mythes mais comment les mythes se pensent dans les hommes, et à leur insu.*" (*Mythologiques* I, p. 20) Native speakers of French disagree as to just what this is intended to mean; and there are two published English versions of this passage. One reads, "We are not, therefore, claiming to show how men think the myths, but rather how the myths think themselves out in men and without men's knowledge."[13] The other reads, "I therefore claim to show, not how men think in myths but how myths operate in men's minds without their being aware of the fact."[14]

The French is ambiguous. "*Comment les mythes se pensent dans les hommes*" might be translated "how myths are thought in men," which would reduce the degree of autonomy implied. The issue of autonomy is important. Lévi-Strauss appears to regard cross-cultural variations of cultural phenomena, especially myth, as self-generated topological distortions of a common structure. As illustration, he refers to D'Arcy Thompson's discussion of the shapes of fish.[15] The presumed au-

---

[13] In Jacques Ehrmann, ed., *Structuralism*, a double issue of *Yale French Studies*, Nos. 36–37 (1966), p. 56; the Introduction to *Mythologiques I* is reprinted there in English translation.

[14] In John and Doreen Weightman, trans., *The Raw and the Cooked* (New York, 1969), p. 12.

[15] See *Mythologiques* IV, p. 606. The last chapter of D'Arcy Thompson, *On Growth and Form* (Cambridge, 1961), is highly relevant for an understanding of Lévi-Strauss' structuralism (Chapter XVII, "On the theory of transformations, or the comparison of related forms").

tonomy implies that Lévi-Strauss can ignore the cultural context of particular variants; the mechanism that generates the observed differences is not that of adaptive evolution or functional relevance, but simply mathematical permutation. The nature of the "human mind," which functions as a kind of randomising computer to generate these permutations "without being aware of the fact," is left obscure. The heresy of Lévi-Strauss' Anglo-Saxon critics is that they start off by assuming that any local variation of a structured form, whether in biology or in culture, is functionally adapted to the local environment, so that we can only claim to understand the local peculiarities after we have taken into account the local environmental circumstances. For such critics, playing tic-tac-toe with topological diagrams is not enough.

However, Lévi-Strauss firmly repudiates the suggestion that he is an idealist, so we have to assume that the somewhat mysterious operations of the "human mind" which he postulates are processes that take place in the ordinary substance of the brain. The implications of his argument seem to be something like this:

In the course of human evolution man has developed the unique capacity to communicate by means of language and signs and not just by means of signals and triggered responses. In order that he should be able to do this it is necessary that the mechanisms of the human brain (which we do not yet understand) embody certain capacities for making plus/minus distinctions, for treating the binary pairs thus formed as related couples, and for manipulating these "relations" as in a matrix algebra. We *know* that the human brain can do this in the case of sound patterns, for structural linguistics has shown that this is one (but only one) essential element in the formation of meaningful speech;

we can therefore postulate that the human brain operates in much the same way when it uses nonverbal elements of culture to form a "sign language" and that the ultimate relational system, the algebra itself, is an attribute of human brains everywhere. But—and this is where the metaphors and the metonyms come in—we also know, not only from the way we can decode speech but more particularly from the way we apprehend music, that the human brain is capable of listening to both harmony and melody at the same time. Now the associations of sounds in harmony—an orchestral score read vertically up and down the page—is metaphoric. In terms of the table on page 49 the notes belong to the system of sounds which can be made by all the assembled orchestral instruments. But the sequence of sounds in a melody—an orchestral score read horizontally across the page—is metonymic. In terms of the table, the notes form a syntagmatic chain derived in sequence from one instrument at a time. So it is Lévi-Strauss' bold proposition that the algebra of the brain can be represented as a rectangular matrix of at least two (but perhaps several) dimensions which can be "read" up and down or side to side like the words of a crossword puzzle. His thesis is that we demonstrably do this with sounds (in the way we listen to words and music); therefore it is intrinsically probable that we also do the same kind of thing when we convey messages by manipulating cultural categories other than sounds.

This is an extreme reductionist argument, but on the face of it, it should help to explain not only how cultural symbols convey messages within a particular cultural milieu but how they convey messages at all. The structure of relations which can be discovered by analyzing materials drawn from any one culture is an algebraic transformation of other possible structures belonging to a common set, and this common set constitutes a pattern which reflects an attribute of the mechanism of all human brains. It is a grand conception; whether it is a useful one may be a matter of opinion.

# The Structure of Myth

## iV

Lévi-Strauss on myth has much the same fascination as Freud on the interpretation of dreams, and the same kind of weaknesses too. A first encounter with Freud is usually persuasive; it is all so neat, it simply must be right. But then you begin to wonder. Supposing the whole Freudian argument about symbolic associations and layers of conscious, unconscious, and preconscious were entirely false, would it ever be possible to *prove* that it is false? And if the answer to that question is "No," you then have to ask yourself whether psychoanalytic arguments about symbol formation and free association can ever be anything better than clever talk.

Lévi-Strauss' discussions about the structure of myth are certainly very clever talk; whether they are really any more than that still remains to be seen.

Myth is an ill-defined category. Some people use the word as if it meant fallacious history—a story about the past which we know to be false; to say that an event is "mythical" is equivalent to saying that it didn't happen. The theological usage is rather different: myth is a formulation of religious mystery—"the expression of unobservable realities in terms of observable phenomena."[1] This comes close to the anthropologist's usual view that "myth is a sacred tale."

If we accept this latter kind of definition the special quality of myth is not that it is false but that it is divinely true for those who believe but fairy tale for those who do not. The distinction that history is true and myth is false is quite arbitrary. Nearly all human societies possess a corpus of tradition about their own past. It starts, as the Bible starts, with a story of the Creation. This is necessarily mythical in *all* senses of the term. But the Creation stories are followed by legends about the exploits of culture heroes (e.g., King David and King Solomon), which *might* have *some* foundation in "true history," and these in turn lead on to accounts of events which everyone accepts as fully historical because their occurrence has been independently recorded in some other source. The Christian New Testament purports to be history from one point of view and myth from another, and he is a rash man who seeks to draw a sharp line between the two.

Lévi-Strauss has evaded this issue of the relation between myth and history by concentrating his attention on "societies with no history"—that is to say, on peoples such as the Australian Aborigines and the tribal peoples of Brazil, who think of their own society as changeless

[1] J. Schniewind, "A Reply to Bultmann," in *Kerygma and Myth*, ed. H. W. Bartsch (London, 1953), p. 47.

and conceive of time present as a straightforward perpetuation of time past. In Lévi-Strauss' usage, myth has no location in chronological time, but it does have certain characteristics which it shares with dreams and fairy tales. In particular, the distinction between nature and culture which dominates normal human experience largely disappears. In Lévi-Straussian myth men converse with animals or marry animal spouses, they live in the sea or in the sky, they perform feats of magic as a matter of course.

Here, as elsewhere, Lévi-Strauss' ultimate concern is with "the unconscious nature of collective phenomena." (*Structural Anthropology*, p. 18) Like Freud he seeks to discover principles of thought formation which are universally valid for all human minds. These universal principles (if they exist) are operative in our brains just as much as in the brains of South American Indians, but in our case the cultural training we have received through living in a high-technology society and through attending school or university has overlaid the universal logic of primitive thought with all kinds of special logics required by the artificial conditions of our social environment. If we are to get at the primitive, universal logic in its uncontaminated form, we need to examine the thought processes of very primitive, technologically unsophisticated peoples (such as the South American Indians), and the study of myth is one way of achieving this end.

Even if we accept the general proposition that there must be a kind of universal inbuilt logic of a nonrational kind which is shared by all humanity and which is made manifest in primitive mythology, we are still faced with many methodological difficulties. Mythology (in Lévi-Strauss' sense) starts out as an oral tradition associated with religious ritual. The tales themselves are usually transmitted in exotic languages at enormous length. By the time they become available to Lévi-Strauss or to any other would-be analyst, they have been written down and transcribed, in abbreviated form, into one or other of the common European languages. In the process they have been completely divorced from their original religious context. This is just as true of the stories which Lévi-Strauss discusses in *Mythologiques* as it is of the myths of Greece and Rome and ancient Scandinavia with which we are more familiar. Even so, Lévi-Strauss asserts that the stories will have retained the essential *structural* characteristics they possessed in the first place, so that if we go about it in the right way a comparison of these emasculated stories can still be made to exhibit the outstanding characteristics of a universal primitive nonrational logic.

Our valuation of such an improbable credo can only be assessed in operational terms. If, by applying Lévi-Strauss' techniques of analysis to an actual body of anthropological materials, we are able to arrive at insights which we did not have before, and these insights throw illumination on other related ethnographic facts which we had not considered in the first instance, then we may feel that the exercise has been worth while. Let me say at once that in many cases there *is* a pay-off of this kind.

The problem, as Lévi-Strauss sees it, is roughly this. If we consider any corpus of mythological tales at their face value we get the impression of an enormous variety of trivial incident, associated with a great deal of repetition and a recurrent harping on very elementary themes —incest between brother and sister or mother and son, parricide and fratricide, cannibalism. . . . Lévi-Strauss postulates that behind the manifest sense of the stories there must be another non-sense (see above, page 29), a message in code. In other words he assumes with Freud that a myth is a kind of collective dream and that it should be capable of interpretation so as to reveal the hidden meaning.

Lévi-Strauss' ideas about the nature of the code and the kind of interpretation that might be possible have several sources.

The first of these comes from Freud: myths express unconscious wishes which are somehow inconsistent with conscious experience. Among primitive peoples the continuity of the political system is dependent upon the perpetuation of alliances between small groups of kin. These alliances are created and cemented by gifts of women: fathers give away their daughters, brothers give away their sisters. But if men are to give away their women to serve social-political ends they must refrain from keeping these women to themselves for sexual ends. Incest and exogamy are therefore opposite sides of the same penny, and the incest taboo (a rule about sexual behavior) is the cornerstone of society (a structure of social and political relations). This moral principle implies that, in the imaginary initial situation, the First Man should have had a wife who was not his sister. But in that case any story about a First Man or a First Woman must contain a logical contradiction. For if they were brother and sister then we are all the outcome of the primeval incest, but, if they were separate creations, only one of them can be the first human being and the other must be (in some sense) other than human: thus the biblical Eve is of one flesh with Adam and their relations are incestuous, but the nonbiblical Lilith was a demon.[2]

[2] This representation of the incest argument is altogether too "empiricist." For Lévi-Strauss the importance of the distinction exogamy/incest is that it marks the establishment

Another contradiction of a comparable kind is that the concept of life entails the concept of death. A living thing is that which is not dead; a dead thing is that which is not alive. But religion endeavors to separate these two intrinsically interdependent concepts so that we have myths which account for the *origin* of death or which represent death as "the gateway to eternal life." Lévi-Strauss has argued that when we are considering the universalist aspects of primitive mythology we shall repeatedly discover that the hidden message is concerned with the resolution of unwelcome contradictions of this sort. The repetitions and prevarications of mythology so fog the issue that irresolvable logical

---

of a social dichotomy order/disorder. The key myth of *Mythologiques I*, M. 1 (pp. 43 ff.) and the key myth of *Mythologiques IV*, M. 529/30 (pp. 25 ff.; 564) are both manifestly "about" incest. They are also both manifestly "about" bird nesting. The bird-nesting element entails suspension in a void between this world and the other, regression to infancy, deprivation from cooked food. Although most of the other details are quite different, Lévi-Strauss declares that the two myths are *identical* but *inverse*. In M. 1 a naked adolescent boy commits incest with his mother, acquires clothing, and, after adventures, kills his father; in M. 529/30 the father of a richly clothed adult son strips the son of his clothing and commits incest with one of the son's many wives. In the course of adventures the son is reborn in an abnormal manner. The father is again destroyed by the son. It is only after extended analysis that these stories can be shown to be concerned with the beginning of society because they are also concerned with the beginning of time, the beginning of order, the beginning of culture. For Lévi-Strauss, the most persistently recurrent "opposition" in mythology is that between order and disorder, but it takes on endless permutations of empirical form. To illustrate this point he places near the end of *Mythologiques I* (p. 318) a series of myths which move from "noisemaking to eclipses, from eclipses to incest, from incest to unruliness, and from unruliness to the coloured plumage of birds." The transformations I offer in the following pages are of a more pedestrian kind.

inconsistencies are lost sight of even when they are openly expressed. In "La Geste d'Asdiwal" (1960), which is, for many people, the most satisfying of all Lévi-Strauss' essays in myth analysis, his conclusion is that:

> All the paradoxes conceived by the native mind, on the most diverse planes: geographic, economic, sociological, and even cosmological, are, when all is said and done, assimilated to that less obvious yet so real paradox which marriage with the matrilateral cousin attempts but fails to resolve. But the failure is *admitted* in our myths, and there precisely lies their function. ("The Story of Asdiwal," pp. 27–28)

But the "admission" is of a complex kind, and even Lévi-Strauss needs two pages of close argument to persuade the reader (who is already in possession of all the relevant evidence) that this is what in fact the myths are saying.

The second major source of Lévi-Strauss thinking on this topic comes from arguments taken over from the field of general information theory. Myth is not just fairy tale; it contains a message. Admittedly, it is not very clear who is sending the message, but it is clear who is receiving it. The novices of the society who hear the myths for the first time are being indoctrinated by the bearers of tradition—a tradition which, in theory at any rate, has been handed down from long-dead ancestors. Let us then think of the ancestors (A) as senders and the present generation (B) as receivers.

Now let us imagine the situation of an individual A who is trying to get a message to a friend B who is almost out of earshot, and let us suppose that communication is further hampered by various kinds of interference—noise from wind, passing cars, and so on.

What will A do? If he is sensible he will not be satisfied with shouting his message just once; he will shout it several times, and give a different wording to the message each time, supplementing his words with visual signals. At the receiving end B may very likely get the meaning of each of the individual messages slightly wrong, but when he puts them together the redundancies and the mutual consistencies and inconsistencies will make it quite clear what is "really" being said.

Suppose, for example, that the intended message consists of eight elements, and that each time that A shouts across to B different parts of that message are obliterated by interference from other noises; then the total pattern of what B receives will consist of a series of "chords" as in an orchestra score, thus:

$$
\begin{array}{cccccccc}
1 & 2 & & 4 & & & 7 & 8 \\
& 2 & 3 & 4 & & 6 & & 8 \\
1 & & & 4 & 5 & & 7 & 8 \\
1 & 2 & & & 5 & & 7 & \\
& & 3 & 4 & 5 & 6 & & 8 \\
\end{array}
$$

Lévi-Strauss' postulate is that a corpus of mythology constitutes an orchestral score of this sort. The collectivity of the senior members of the society, through its religious institutions, is unconsciously transmitting to the junior members a basic message which is manifest in the score as a whole rather than in any particular myth.

Many social anthropologists of the more usual Anglo-American sort—the functionalists of whom Lévi-Strauss is so critical—are prepared to go along with him this far, but they find his method far less acceptable whenever he ignores the cultural limitations of time and space.

In "The Story of Asdiwal," Lévi-Strauss devotes forty

pages to the analysis of a single complex of myths precisely located in a particular cultural region, and the
result is entirely fascinating. But when, like Frazer, he
roams about among the ethnographies of the whole
world picking up odd details of custom and story to
reveal what he presumes to be a single unitary message
inherent in the architecture of the human mind, most
of his British admirers get left behind. Here is an example of this latter procedure: "As in archaic China and
certain Amerindian societies there was until recently
a European custom which entailed the ritual extinction
and subsequent rekindling of domestic hearths preceded
by fasting and by the use of instruments of darkness
[*instruments des tenèbres*]." (*Mythologiques II*, p. 351)
"Instruments of darkness" refers to a twelfth-century
European custom in which, between Good Friday and
Easter Eve, the ordinary church bells were silent and
were replaced by various other noise-producing devices,
the din from which was supposed to remind the faithful
of the prodigies and terrifying sounds which accompanied the death of Christ. (*Mythologiques II*, p. 348)
In the cited quotation Lévi-Strauss has given this
medieval European Christian category a world-wide extension by using it to include any kind of musical instrument which is employed as a signal to mark the
beginning or end of a ritual performance. He then draws
attention to the use of such signals in various situations
where lights and fires are extinguished and rekindled
at the beginning and end of a period of fast. And finally
he comes back to Europe and notes that "instruments
of darkness" are used in contexts of the latter kind.
The whole argument is circular, since the universality
of the conjunction of "instruments of darkness" and
fasting is already presupposed in the operational definition of the terms employed.

Very substantial sections of all four volumes of *Mythologiques* are open to objections of this kind, and, to be frank, this grand-scale survey of the mythology of the Americas, which extends to two thousand pages and gives details of eight hundred and thirteen different stories and their variants, often degenerates into a latter-day *Golden Bough,* with all the methodological defects which such a comment might imply. Lévi-Strauss is, of course, well aware that he is open to criticism of this kind, and in *Mythologiques III* (pp. 11–12) he goes to some lengths to justify an astonishing claim that a Tukuna myth which is "impossible to interpret" in its native South American context becomes comprehensible when brought into association with a "paradigmatic system" drawn from the myths of North America. It seems to me that only the most uncritical devotees are likely to be persuaded by this argument. But, even so, the structural analysis of myth deserves our serious attention. Just what does this expression mean?

I shall try to explain by demonstration, but I must emphasize two preliminary points. First, a full exposition of the method requires a great deal of space; my skeletal examples give no indication of the subtleties of the technique. Second, Lévi-Strauss' method is not entirely new. In England, Hocart and Lord Raglan made gropings in the same direction over forty years ago; so did the Russian folklorist Vladimir Propp.[3] Rather later, Georges Dumezil, one of Lévi-Strauss' senior colleagues at the Collège de France, began to develop ideas

---

[3] See Claude Lévi-Strauss, "La Structure et la forme. Réflexions sur un ouvrage de Vladimir Propp," in *Cahiers de l'Institut des Sciences économiques appliquées* (Paris), 1960.

which run parallel to those of Lévi-Strauss in quite a number of ways. But the latter has carried the theoretical analysis of what he is up to much further than any of the others.

In Lévi-Strauss' first essay on this topic[4] he uses, as one of his examples, an abbreviated analysis of the structure of the Oidipus story. This is one of the very few cases in which he has so far applied his method to a myth which is likely to be familiar to an English or American reader, so let us start with that. I have followed Lévi-Strauss fairly closely, introducing modifications only at points where his argument seems particularly obscure.

He first assumes that the myth (any myth) can readily be broken up into segments or incidents, and that everyone familiar with the story will agree as to what these incidents are. The incidents in every case refer to the "relations" between the individual characters in the story, or to the "status" of particular individuals. These relations and statuses are the points on which we need to focus our attention; the individual characters, as such, as often interchangeable.

In the particular case of the Oidipus[5] myth he takes the following segments of a syntagmatic chain:

   i. "Kadmos seeks his sister Europe, ravished by Zeus."
   ii. "Kadmos kills the Dragon."

[4] Claude Lévi-Strauss, "The Structural Study of Myth," *Journal of American Folklore*, Vol. 68, No. 270 (1955).
[5] In this and subsequent stories I use an anglicized Greek (rather than a Latin) spelling of personal names in the form in which they appear in the Index of H. J. Rose, *A Handbook of Greek Mythology* (1959). A summary of the leading features of the Theban myth cycle is given below, pages 78 ff.

iii. "The Spartoi (the men who are born as a result
of sowing the dragon's teeth) kill one another."

iv. "Oidipus kills his father Laios."

v. "Oidipus kills the Sphinx." (But in fact, in the
story, the Sphinx commits suicide after Oidipus
has answered the riddle.)

vi. "Oidipus marries his mother Jokaste."

vii. "Eteokles kills his brother Polyneikes."

viii. "Antigone buries her brother Polyneikes despite
prohibition."

Lévi-Strauss also draws our attention to a peculiarity of
three of the names:

ix. Labdakos (father of Laios)= "Lame"

x. Laios (father of Oidipus)  = "Left-sided"

xi. Oidipus                   = "Swollen-foot"

Lévi-Strauss admits that the selection of these characters and these incidents is to some extent arbitrary,
but he argues that if we added more incidents they
would only be variations of the ones we have already.
This is true enough. For example: Oidipus' task is to
kill the Sphinx; he does this by answering the riddle:
the answer to the riddle, according to some authorities,
was "the child grows into an adult who grows into an
old man"; the Sphinx then commits suicide; Oidipus
("the child grown into an adult") then marries his
mother, Jokaste; when Oidipus learns the answer to
this riddle, Jokaste commits suicide and Oidipus puts
out his own eyes to become an old man. So also, if we
were to pursue the fortunes of Antigone, we should note
that, having "buried" her dead brother in defiance of
the command of her mother's brother (Kreon), she is
in turn herself buried alive by Kreon; she commits
suicide; her suicide is followed by that of her betrothed
cousin Haimon and also that of Haimon's mother
Eurydike.

But where should we stop? In another version Haimon is killed by the Sphinx; in another Antigone bears Haimon a son who is killed by Kreon, and so on.

So let us stick to Lévi-Strauss' own skeletal version. He puts his eleven segments into four columns, thus:

| I | II | III | IV |
|---|---|---|---|
| (i) Kadmos/ Europe | | (ii) Kadmos/ Dragon | |
| | (iii) Spartoi | | |
| | (iv) Oidipus/ Laios | | (ix) Lame Labdakos |
| (vi) Oidipus/ Jokaste | | (v) Oidipus/ Sphinx | |
| | (vii) Eteokles/ Poly- neikes | | (x) Left-sided Laios |
| (viii) Anti- gone/ Poly- neikes | | | (xi) Swollen- footed Oidipus |

He then points out that in each of the incidents in Column I there is a ritual offense of the nature of incest —"an overvaluation of kinship." This contrasts with the incidents in Column II, where the offenses are of the nature of fratricide/parricide—"an undervaluation of kinship." In Column III the common element is the destruction of anomalous monsters by men, while Column IV refers to men who are themselves to some extent anomalous monsters. Here Lévi-Strauss introjects a general proposition based on grand-scale comparative ethnography of the Frazerian kind: "In mythology it is a universal characteristic of men born from the Earth that at the moment they emerge from the depth they either cannot walk or they walk clumsily. This is the case of the chthonian beings in the mythology of the Pueblo . . . [and of] the Kwakiutl." This, so he says, explains the peculiarity of the names.

Anyway, the nature of the anomalous monsters in Column III is that they are half man–half animal, and the story of the sowing of the dragon's teeth implies a doctrine of the autochthonous origin of man; the Spartoi were born from the earth without human aid. In contrast, the story of Oidipus' being exposed at birth and staked to the ground (this was the origin of his swollen foot) implies that even though born of woman he was not fully separated from his natural earth. And so, says Lévi-Strauss, Column III, in which the monsters are overcome, signifies *denial of the autochthonous origin of man*, while Column IV signifies the *persistence of the autochthonous origin of man*. So IV is the converse of III just as II is the converse of I!

By this hair-splitting logic we end up with an equation:

$$I/II : : III/IV$$

But Lévi-Strauss maintains that there is more to this than algebra. The formal religious theory of the Greeks was that man was autochthonous. The first man was half a serpent; he grew from the earth as plants grow from the earth. Therefore the puzzle that needs to be solved is:

how to find a satisfactory transition between this theory and the knowledge that human beings are actually born from the union of man and woman. Although the problem obviously cannot be solved, the Oidipus myth provides a kind of logical tool which relates to the original problem—born from one or born from two—to the derivative problem: born from different or born from the same. By a correlation of this type, "the overrating of blood relations" is to the "underrating of blood relations" as "the attempt to escape autochthony" is to the "impossibility to succeed in it." Although experience contradicts theory, social life validates cosmology by its similarity of structure. Hence, cosmology is true. (*Structural Anthropology*, p. 216)[6]

Those who think that all this is vaguely reminiscent of an argument from *Alice through the Looking Glass* will not be far wrong. Lewis Carroll, in his *alter ego* as mathematician, was one of the originators of the peculiar kind of binary logic upon which Lévi-Straussian discourse and modern computer technology are alike constructed.

It must be admitted that, emasculated in this way, the argument almost ceases to be comprehensible, yet even so, the reader may suspect that behind the nonsense there is a sense. The reason why Lévi-Strauss has not pursued his explorations of classical Greek mythology any further seems to be that, in the somewhat bowdlerized form in which these stories have come down to us, there are too few parameters. The South American mythology, which has provided the main arena of his explorations, has many more dimensions. In particular he is there able to show that:

1. sets of relationships among human beings in

---

[6] Compare also the following quotations: "The purpose of myth is to provide a logical model capable of overcoming a contradiction (an impossible achievement if, as it happens, the contradiction is real)." And, "The inability to connect two kinds of relationships is overcome (or rather replaced) by the assertion that the contradictory relationships are identical inasmuch as they are both self-contradictory in a similar way." (*Structural Anthropology*, pp. 229, 216)

　　　　terms of relative status, friendship and hostility,
　　　　sexual availability, mutual dependence

may be represented in myth, either in direct or transposed form, as

2.　relationships among different kinds (species) of
　　men, animals, birds, reptiles, insects, supernatural
　　beings

3.　relationships between categories of food and
　　modes of food preparation and the use or non-use
　　of fire (above, page 27)

4.　relations between categories of sound and silence
　　produced either naturally as animal cries or arti-
　　ficially by means of musical instruments

5.　relations between categories of smell and taste—
　　pleasant/unpleasant, sweet/sour, etc.

6.　relations between types of human dress and un-
　　dress and between the animals and plants from
　　which the clothing is derived

7.　relations between body functions: e.g., eating,
　　excretion, urination, vomiting, copulation, birth,
　　menstruation

8.　relations between categories of landscape, sea-
　　sonal change, climate, time alternations, celestial
　　bodies

or combinations of any of these. The main purpose of
his South American analysis is not merely to show that
such symbolization occurs, for Freud and his followers
have already claimed to demonstrate this, but to show
that the transformations follow strictly logical rules.

Lévi-Strauss displays quite extraordinary ingenuity
in the way he exhibits this hidden logic, but the argument is extremely complicated and very difficult to
evaluate.

Is it possible to present a reduced model of such a
system of analysis and still convey the general sense?

In his original article Lévi-Strauss remarks at the end of his brief discussion of Oidipus:

> If a myth is made up of all its variants, structural analysis should take them all into account. After analyzing all the known variants of the Theban version, we should thus treat the others in the same way: first the tales about Labdakos' collateral line including Agave, Pentheus, and Jokaste herself; the Theban version about Lykos with Amphion and Zetos as the city founders; more remote variants concerning Dionysos (Oidipus' matrilateral cousin) and Athenian legends where Kekrops takes the place of Kadmos. For each of them a similar chart should be drawn and then compared and reorganized according to the findings. (*Structural Anthropology*, p. 217)

The methodological program applied to American materials in *Mythologiques* is a modification of this plan. Volume I starts with a Bororo myth from South America (M. 1) and explores variants and permutations. There is recurrent emphasis on the theme that "culinary operations are viewed as mediatory activities between heaven and earth, life and death, nature and society." Volume II examines more convoluted versions of the same complex, and Volume III pursues the chase into North America. Volume IV leads us the other way round: starting with a myth from the American Northwest (M. 529), variants eventually take us back to South America. The emphasis on cooking as an agent of transformation persists, but the title *Naked Man* draws attention to the recurrent equivalence: naked/clothed = Nature/Culture. At the end of the day Lévi-Strauss claims to have demonstrated that the whole vast agglomeration of stories forms a single system. In principle, such an operation might be expanded indefinitely so there can be nothing heretical about applying the rules of the game to the mythology of Classical Greece. There are indeed striking American parallels for some well-known European themes.[7]

In particular, Orpheus, being heavily laden with binary antitheses, seems positively to invite a Lévi-Straussian investigation:

> He is a son of gentle Apollo but a follower of wild Dionysos, with whom he becomes identified.
>
> He rescues his wife from the land of the dead by means of music but loses her because of silence— "not hearing her footsteps behind him."
>
> He is a devoted husband yet the originator of male homosexuality; his oracle was located on Lesbos, the traditional source of female homosexuality.

Furthermore, the Orpheus-Euridike story is a structural permutation of the Demeter-Persephone story:

> Euridike the wife and Persephone the Virgin Daughter are both carried off to rule as Queen of the Underworld.
>
> Orpheus the husband fails to rescue his wife and is sterile; Demeter the mother partially rescues her daughter and is fertile.
>
> Euridike dies in consequence of being bitten by a snake while evading the sexual embraces of Aristaios, half-brother to Orpheus. The punishment of Aristaios is that he loses his bees and hence his *honey*. He recovers his bees by finding a swarm in the carcass of a sacrificed animal which has been specially allowed to go *putrid* instead of being *cooked and burned* for the gods in the usual way. Persephone fails to achieve immortality because she eats *raw* pomegranate seeds in the other world; her foster

[7] See A. Hultkrantz, *The North American Indian Orpheus Tradition* (New York, 1958).

brother Demophoon nearly achieves immortality because he eats nothing in this world but is instead anointed with ambrosia, a food of the gods related to honey. He fails to achieve immortality because his real mother (Metaneira) drags him from fire in which he is being *cooked* by Demeter, who is seeking to burn away his mortality. Persephone is lured to her doom by the fragrant smell of fresh flowers.

Already I have started enough hares to fill a whole volume of Lévi-Strauss' *magnum opus*, and our author himself is undoubtedly aware of the possibilities (see, e.g., *Mythologiques II*, p. 347). But the ordinary reader who is unfamiliar with the details of classical mythology or the permutations and combinations in *Mythologiques* can hardly be expected to decipher such a rigmarole. I shall attempt something much more modest. By following through a very restricted version of Lévi-Strauss' original plan, I shall try to give the reader some feeling of how, in a structuralist analysis, the contrasted patterns of superficially different stories can be seen to fit together. It needs to be realized, however, that in any such truncated illustration we necessarily forfeit many of the subtler nuances of the technique.

Within these limitations the analysis which follows, which discusses eight stories in outline and mentions several others in skeletal form, is intended to illustrate certain key features in Lévi-Strauss' procedure. The various stories are all summarized in the same way so that the roles of the various *dramatis personae* can be easily distinguished. King, Queen, Mother, Father, Brother, Sister, Daughter, Son, Son-in-law, Paramour, etc., are seen to exhibit permutations of a single "plot."

The comparison rests on a basic underlying hypothesis to the effect that Greek mythology as a whole constitutes a single "system" (language) and that each individual story is a syntagm of that system (pages 48–50). The system as a whole presupposes a certain metaphorical apprehension of the relative positions of men and animals and deities in a matrix formed by the oppositions:

ABOVE/BELOW, THIS WORLD/OTHER WORLD,
CULTURE/NATURE

This schema is summarized below in Figure 5. Other factors which are presupposed in my analysis (this would be more evident if my description of the myths were more complete) are the transformational rules hinted at in my remarks about the Orpheus story (page 74). The Greek deities were supposed to eat only fresh uncooked foods—ambrosia, nectar, honey—but they delighted in the smell of burnt offerings. Thus BURNING/PUTRID :: SKY/UNDERWORLD. In my versions of the myths the issue is blatantly about sex and homicide;

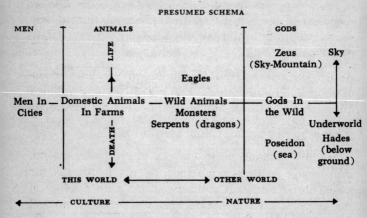

*Figure 5*

in a fuller account it would be seen that this issue also appears in other guises transposed onto other planes. Just *how* this works cannot be shown in brief space, but the following generalization by Lévi-Strauss derived from his American material may well apply to the Greek data also:

> [There is] an analogy between honey and menstrual blood. Both are transformed (*élaborée*) substances resulting from a sort of *infra-cuisine*, vegetal in the one case . . . animal in the other. Moreover, honey may be either healthy or toxic, just as a woman in her normal condition is a "honey", but secretes a poison when she is indisposed. Finally we have seen that, in native thought, the search for honey represents a sort of return to Nature, in the guise of erotic attraction transposed from the sexual register to that of the sense of taste which undermines the very foundations of Culture if it is indulged in for too long. In the same way the *honey*-moon will be a menace to public order if the bridal pair are allowed to extend their private game indefinitely and to neglect their duties to society. (*Mythologiques III*, p. 340)

And if the relevance of all this to what follows seems obscure I can only remark that one of the unmentioned characters, Glaukos, son of Minos and brother-in-law to Dionysos, was "drowned in a jar of honey" and re-born from a tomb.

Finally, I should point out that the ultimate conclusion of the analysis is not that "all the myths say the same thing" but that "collectively the sum of what all the myths say is not expressly said by any of them, and that what they thus say (collectively) is a necessary poetic truth which is an unwelcome contradiction." It

is Lévi-Strauss' thesis that the function of mythology is
to exhibit publicly, though in disguise, ordinarily unconscious paradoxes of this kind (*cf.* page 63). The
underlying assumption throughout the analysis is that
this "reduced model," which arranges various pairs of
categories in binary opposition along two axes, is implicit in the whole system of mythology of which the
listed stories are particular examples.


# THE STORIES

1 / *Kadmos, Europe, and the Dragon's Teeth*

> *Story:* Zeus (God) in the form of a tame wild
> bull (mediator between wild and tame) seduces
> and carries off a human girl, Europe.
>
> Europe's brother, Kadmos, and mother, Tele-
> phassa, search for her. The mother dies and is
> buried by Kadmos. Kadmos is then told to follow a
> particular cow (domestic animal: replacement of
> the sister and the mother). Where the cow stops,
> Kadmos must found Thebes, having first sacrificed
> the cow to Athena. (Cow forms link between man
> and gods just as bull formed link between gods
> and man.) In seeking to provide water for the
> sacrifice Kadmos encounters a dragon (monster)
> guarding a sacred pool. The dragon is a son of
> Ares, god of war. Kadmos and the dragon engage
> in battle. Having killed the dragon, Kadmos sows
> the dragon's teeth (a domestic action applied to
> wild material). The crop is men (the Spartoi)
> without mothers. They kill one another, but the
> survivors cooperate with Kadmos to found Thebes.
> Kadmos makes peace with Ares and marries his

daughter Harmonia. The gods give Harmonia a magical necklace as dowry, which later brings disaster to everyone who possesses it. At the end of the story Kadmos and Harmonia change into dragons.

*Comment:* The story specifies the polarity Nature : Culture :: Gods : Men and affirms that the relationship between gods and men is one of ambiguous and unstable alliance—exemplified by marriage followed by feud followed by marriage accompanied by poisoned marriage gifts. There is also the ambiguity of autochthony/nonautochthony. Kadmos, who slays the dragon from whom are born the Spartoi, is himself the dragon and ancestor of the Spartoi.

## 2 / Minos and the Minotaur

*Story:* Minos is son of Zeus and Europe (story 1) and husband to Pasiphaë, daughter of the Sun.

Poseidon is brother to Zeus but his counterpart, god of the sea instead of god of the sky.

Poseidon sends Minos a beautiful bull which should be sacrificed; Minos retains the bull. In punishment Poseidon causes Pasiphaë to lust after the bull. By the ingenuity of Daidalos, Pasiphaë is changed into a cow and has sex relations with the bull, of which union is born the monster Minotaur, who annually devours a tribute of living youths and maidens.

*Comment:* This is the inverse of story 1, thus:
(a) *Kadmos version:* Bull (Zeus) carries away Europe, who has a human child, Minos. Europe has a human brother, Kadmos, who is required to sacrifice a cow, sent from the

gods, and in the process he kills a monster from whose remains come live human beings. But Kadmos is himself the monster.

(b) *Minos version:* Bull (Poseidon) cohabits with Pasiphaë, who has a monster child, Minotaur. Pasiphaë has a human husband, Minos, who is required to sacrifice a bull, sent from the gods (which he fails to do). The bull is replaced by a monster who consumes human beings. But the monster = Minotaur = Minos–Bull is himself Minos.

In effect, the two stories have almost identical "structures"; one story is converted into the other by "changing the signs"—i.e., bulls become cows, brothers become husbands, and so on.

The implication is the same as before. Again we have a polarity Gods : Men :: Wild : Tame :: Monsters : Domestic Animals, with the Divine Bull an ambiguous creature linking the two sides. Again sexual relations between gods and men and the sacrifice of divine animals expresses the highly equivocal alliance in which the friendship of the gods is bought only at enormous cost.

### 3 / Theseus, Ariadne, and the Minotaur

*Story:* Theseus, son of Poseidon by a human mother, is ranged against Minos, son of Zeus by a human mother. Ariadne, daughter of Minos and Pasiphaë (story 2), loves Theseus and betrays her father by means of a *thread*. Theseus kills the Minotaur and elopes with Ariadne but deserts her.

*Comment:* This is one of a group of closely related stories in which a father or the father's double (here Minos–Minotaur) is killed by his enemy because of the treachery of the daughter, who loves the enemy; but the victorious enemy then punishes the daughter by desertion or murder. Thus:

(a) Minos is at war with Nisos, King of Megara, a descendant of the autochthonous Kekrops. Nisos is preserved from death by a magic lock of *hair*. Skylla, daughter of Nisos, cuts off the hair and presents it as a love token to Minos. Minos kills Nisos but abandons Skylla in disgust. Nisos is then turned into a sea eagle in perpetual pursuit of his errant daughter in the form of another sea bird (*keiris*).

(b) Perseus, son of Zeus by the human Danaë, is founder-King of Mycenae. The kingdom passes to Perseus' son Alkaios and then to Elektryon, brother of Alkaios, who engages in feud with Pterelaos, grandson of Nestor, another brother of Alkaios. Amphitryon, son of Alkaios, is betrothed to Alkmene, daughter of Elektryon (his father's brother). Elektryon gives Amphitryon the kingdom but binds him by oath not to sleep with Alkmene until vengeance against Pterelaos has been achieved.

In the course of the feud the sons of Pterelaos drive off Elektryon's *cows* and are counterattacked by the sons of Elektryon. One son from each side survives. Amphitryon redeems the cattle but, as he is driving them home, one of the cows runs aside. Amphitryon flings a stick at the cow but the stick hits Elektryon, who is killed. Pterelaos is, like Nisos, preserved from death by a magic *hair*. Komaitho, daughter of Pterelaos, in love with Amphitryon, betrays her father [as in (a)]. Amphitryon kills Pterelaos but also kills Komaitho for her treachery.

Notice, first, that the killing of Elektryon on account of an errant *cow* is metaphoric of the killing of the other fathers on account of an errant *daughter*, and, second, that in each case there is a clash of loyalties, since the daughter must betray the father in seeking to gain a husband. In the first two cases (Theseus, Minos) the potential husband rejects the sinful daughter, but in the third case the "contradiction" is resolved by a duplication of roles. Pterelaos is the double of Elektryon, Komaitho is the double of Alkmene. Amphitryon kills both the fathers, but his killing of Komaitho allows him to marry Alkmene.

(c) Alkmene now becomes the prototype of the faithful wife. Nevertheless she is faithless, since she becomes the mother of Herakles as the result of sexual union with Zeus, who had impersonated her husband Amphitryon.

These stories add up to a variation of Lévi-Strauss' generalization cited on page 69. The hero who is left on stage (Theseus in the one case, Herakles in the other) is the son of a human mother by a divine father and therefore the opposite of the autochthonous beings (such as Kekrops) who are born of the earth without reference to women. Yet Lévi-Strauss' formula still applies, except that the problem of incest ("the overrating of blood relations") and parricide/fratricide ("the underrating of blood relations") is replaced by the problem of exogamy and feud ("the overrating of affinal relations"—treachery by the errant daughter —and "the underrating of affinal relations"— murder of the potential father-in-law by the potential son-in-law).

## 4 / Antiope, Zethos, and Amphion

*Story:* Kadmos is succeeded as King of Thebes, first by a daughter's son, Pentheus, then by his own son, Polydoros, then by Labdakos, son of Polydoros. Pentheus and Labdakos both become sacrifices to Dionysos—their womenfolk in a frenzy mistake them for wild beasts and tear them to pieces. Laios, the next heir, is an infant, and the throne is usurped by Lykos, Labdakos' mother's father's brother. Antiope, daughter of Nykteus, is brother's daughter to Lykos. She becomes pregnant by Zeus. Nykteus, dishonored, commits suicide, and the duty of punishing Antiope for her liaison falls on Lykos. Lykos and his wife, Dirke, capture and imprison Antiope, but not before she has given birth to twins, Zethos (a warrior) and Amphion (a musician), who as infants are exposed on a mountain and (like Oidipus) rescued by shepherds. In due course the twins discover their mother and avenge themselves on Lykos and Dirke and reign jointly in Thebes.

*Comment:* This story combines features from story 3 with those of the better-known Oidipus stories (6 and 7 below). The role of Amphitryon in 3 (b) is taken over by Zeus. The suicide of Nykteus is, in effect, a slaying of the father-in-law by the son-in-law. Zethos and Amphion are sons of Zeus by a human mother; their opponent, Lykos, is son of the autochthonous Chthonios. In other respects Antiope is a sort of Antigone-Jokaste. Antiope, like Antigone, is imprisoned by her uncle, but where Lykos is father's brother of Antiope, Kreon is mother's brother of Antigone. Amphion and Zethos resemble Oidipus in that they are exposed on a mountain in childhood and seize the throne after killing the king. But they kill the king after discovering their true parentage, whereas Oidipus kills the king first. They also resemble Eteokles and Polyneikes in that they are twins who both claim the throne, but they rule together in amity, one as a warrior and one as a musician, whereas the Argives, both being warriors, kill one another. Like Oidipus, Amphion and Zethos are "mediators" between the sky gods and the underworld in that their mother Antiope is in the line of Chthonios and their father is Zeus.

So far as the succession principle is concerned Amphion and Zethos are the opposites of the Spartoi. The Spartoi are the autochthonous sons of a Chthonian man-monster, Kadmos; Amphion and Zethos are the sons of a human mother by a sky-deity, Zeus. But the final outcome is disaster. Amphion marries Niobe, by whom he has many children, but Niobe boasts of her fertility and the whole family is destroyed by the wrath of the gods.

*Moral:* Amity between brothers (Amphion-Zethos) is ultimately no more fruitful than fratricide (Eteokles-Polyneikes).

## 5 / Theseus, Phaidra, and Hippolytos

*Story:* Hippolytos is the son of Theseus by Antiope, Queen of the Amazons. Phaidra, daughter of Minos, is wife to Theseus and step-mother to Hippolytos. Phaidra falls in love with Hippolytos, who rejects her advances; Phaidra then accuses Hippolytos of having tried to rape her. In revenge Theseus appeals to Poseidon to slay Hippolytos, and Hippolytos dies. Phaidra commits suicide. Theseus discovers his error and suffers remorse.

*Comment:* This is very close to being the inverse of the Oidipus story (7). Here the father kills the son instead of the son killing the father. The son does not sleep with the mother, though he is accused of doing so. The mother commits suicide in both cases; the surviving father-son suffers remorse in both cases. It will be observed that the failure of Hippolytos to commit incest with his (step-) mother Phaidra has an even more negative outcome than the actual incest of Oidipus with Jokaste.

Notice further that Phaidra is sister to Ariadne (story 3). The roles are now reversed. Instead of the son-in-law killing the father-in-law because of the treachery of the daughter, the father kills the son because of the treachery of the mother.

## 6 / Laios, Chrysippos, and Jokaste

*Story:* During the reign of Lykos, Amphion, and Zethos, Laios goes into banishment and is befriended by Pelops. He falls in love with Pelops' son, Chrysippos, whom he teaches to drive a chariot. After returning to the throne of Thebes he marries Jokaste but avoids sleeping with her because of the prophecy that her son will kill him. The conception which results in the birth of Oidipus follows a bout of lust when Laios has got drunk at a religious feast. On the occasion when he encountered Oidipus "at the crossroads," Oidipus was a "young man driving a chariot."

*Comment:* The myth establishes an equivalence between Chrysippos and Oidipus, and the incest between Oidipus and his mother is matched by homosexual incest between Laios and his son.

## 7 / *Oidipus*

*Story:* The King (Laios) and the Queen (Jokaste) rule in Thebes. The son (Oidipus) is exposed on a mountain with his ankles staked and thought to be dead. He survives. The son meets the King-father "at a crossroads" and kills him. The Queen's brother (Kreon) acts as regent. Thebes is beset by a monster (Sphinx: female). The Queen's hand in marriage is offered to anyone who will get rid of the monster by answering its riddle. Oidipus does so. The monster commits suicide. The son assumes all aspects of the deceased father's role. On discovery, the Queen commits suicide; son-King (Oidipus) blinds himself and becomes a seer (acquires supernatural sight).

## 8 / *Argives (Antigone, Eteokles, and Polyneikes)*

*Story:* Oidipus has two sons, Eteokles and Polyneikes, who are also his half-brothers, since they are sons of Jokaste. Oidipus having abdicated, Eteokles and Polyneikes are supposed to hold the throne alternately. Eteokles takes the throne first and refuses to give it up; Polyneikes is banished and leads an army of heroes from Argos against Thebes. The expedition fails. Eteokles and Polyneikes kill each other. Antigone, in defiance of Kreon, performs funeral rites over Polyneikes. In punishment she is walled up alive in a tomb, where she commits suicide. Later the sons of the dead heroes lead another expedition against Thebes and are triumphant.

   *Comment:* Lévi-Strauss' own treatment of stories 7 and 8 in conjunction with story 1 has already been given on pages 67–71.

It will be seen that if we proceed in this way there never comes a point at which we can say that we have considered "all the variants," for almost any story drawn from the general complex of classical Greek mythology turns out to be a variant in one way or another. If, for example, we take as our central theme the Oidipus complex as understood by Freud—the story of a son who kills his father and then becomes the paramour of his mother—we shall find that the following well-known stories are all "variants." Thus:

*Oidipus:* son kills father and becomes paramour.

*Agamemnon:* paramour kills father inviting vengeance from the son.

*Odysseus:* father merges with son and destroys the would-be paramours. Odysseus has no descendants.

*Menelaos:* paramour (Paris) is destroyed by a third party and there is no heir (son).

*Hippolytos* (story 5): innocent son, falsely accused of being paramour, is killed by father.

What emerges from such a comparison is that each story is seen to be a combination of relational themes, that each theme is one of a set of variations, and that what is significant about these relational themes is the contrast between the variations.

The message contained in the whole set of stories— the ones I have spelled out at some length and the ones I have mentioned only by title—cannot readily be put into words; otherwise there would be no need for such circumlocution. But, roughly, what it amounts to is simple enough: if society is to go on, daughters must be disloyal to their parents and sons must destroy (replace) their fathers.[8]

Here then is the irresolvable unwelcome contradiction, the necessary fact that we hide from consciousness because its implications run directly counter to the fundamentals of human morality. There are no heroes in these stories; they are simply epics of unavoidable human disaster. The disaster always originates in the circumstances that a human being fails to fulfill his or her proper obligations toward a deity or a kinsman, and this, in part at least, is what Lévi-Strauss is getting at when he insists that the fundamental moral implication of mythology is that "Hell is ourselves," which I take to mean "self-interest is the source of all evil."

But I must again remind the reader that this whole example is Leach imitating Lévi-Strauss and not a summary of a Lévi-Strauss original. It has been necessary to go to this length in order to display the "theme and variations" aspects of a typical Lévi-Straussian analysis, but in all other respects the material is thin and atypical. There is a paucity of magical happenings and a monotonous concentration on the bed-rock issues of homicide

[8] Cf. Lévi-Strauss' own formula, cited on page 69. In my extended analysis Incest : Fratricide-Parricide : : Murder of potential father-in-law : Exogamy : : "born from one" : "born from two" : : Society in which there is no succession (Odysseus) : Society in which there is succession (Oidipus). That the Odyssey has this static implication is confirmed by consideration of a post-Homeric supplement which unsuccessfully attempts to resolve the puzzle by splitting the various roles: Telemachos, son of Odysseus and Penelope, has a half-brother, Telegonos, son of Odysseus and Kirke; Telegonos accidentally kills Odysseus and marries Penelope; Telemachos marries Kirke.

and sexual misdemeanor. In Lévi-Strauss' own examples these ultimate conflicts are usually transformed into a language code of some other kind.

For example, in his American case material many of the most perceptive of Lévi-Strauss' comparisons derive from analogies between eating and sexual intercourse. Close parallels are not easily found in classical mythology, but the stories relating to the ancestry of Zeus, which are themselves in certain respects duplicates of the Oidipus myth, will serve as a partial illustration:

> Gaea, Earth, first produces Uranos, Heaven, by spontaneous generation. Then Uranos copulates with his mother. She bears the Titans. Uranos, jealous of his sons, thrusts them back into the body of their mother. Gaea, unable to tolerate this state of permanent gestation, arms the last of her sons, Kronos, with a sickle with which he castrates his father. The drops of blood fall to earth and turn into the Furies, the Giants, and the Nymphs; the castrated member itself falls to the sea and is transformed into Aphrodite, the goddess of love. Kronos then rules and is in turn told that he will be overthrown by his son, but where Laios tried to save himself by abstaining from heterosexual intercourse (story 6 above) Kronos indulges himself but swallows his children as fast as they are born. When Zeus is born the mother, Rhea, gives Kronos a phallic-shaped stone instead of the newborn babe. Kronos then vomits up the stone along with all the children previously consumed.

In this story, the ordinary act of sexual intercourse is transposed. Where in reality the male inserts a phallus into the female vagina and thereafter children are born through the vagina, in the myth the female inserts a phallus into the male mouth as a form of food and thereafter the children are born through the mouth in the form of vomit. A crude nursery imagery, no doubt, but in Lévi-Strauss' view this exemplifies a very general principle—"In the language [plan] of myth vomit is the correlative and inverse term to coitus and defecation is the correlative and inverse term to auditory communication" (*Mythologiques II*, p. 210)—and by the time he has finished with it, he has linked up this symbolism with modes of cooking, methods of making fire, changes in the seasons, the menstrual periods of young women, the diet of young mothers and elderly spinsters, and Lord knows what else. To discover just how one thing leads to another, however, the reader must pursue some inquiries on his own. Having started at *Mythologiques II* (pp. 210–12), he will be led back to various other Lévi-Straussian references, but notably to *Mythologiques I* (p. 344) and "The Structural Study of Myth," from which we started out. The journey is well worth while, though the traveler will not necessarily be all that the wiser when he comes to the end of it.

Let me say again that even among those who have found it extremely rewarding to apply Lévy-Strauss' structuralist techniques to the detailed study of particular bodies of case material, there is widespread skepticism about the reckless sweep with which he himself is prepared to apply his generalizations. For example, consider the following:

With regard to the riddle of the Sphinx, Lévi-Strauss claims that it is in the nature of things that a mythical riddle should have no answer. It is also in the nature of things that a mother should not marry her own son. Oidipus contradicts nature by answering the riddle; he also contradicts nature by marrying his mother.

Now if we define a mythical riddle as "a question which postulates that there is no answer" then the converse would be "an answer for which there was no question." In the Oidipus stories disaster ensues because someone answers the unanswerable question; in another class of myths of world-wide distribution, disaster ensues because someone fails to ask the answerable question. Lévi-Strauss cites as examples the death of Buddha because Ananda failed to ask him to remain alive and the disasters of the Fisher-King which are the consequence of Gawain-Percival's failing to ask about the nature of the Holy Grail.

This kind of verbal juggling with the generalized formula is quite typical of Lévi-Strauss' hypothesis-forming procedure, but such methods cannot show us the truth; they only lead into a world where all things are possible and nothing sure.

Words and Things

Lévi-Strauss' lively but relatively brief study *La Pensée sauvage* (1962) is related to the massive but meticulously elaborated volumes of *Mythologiques* in much the same way as Freud's *The Psychopathology of Everyday Life* is related to *The Interpretation of Dreams*. In each case the shorter work endeavors to relate some of the findings of the more formal academic study to "ordinary experience." *La Pensée sauvage*, it is true, often strays a long way from ordinary experience; neither totemism nor existentialism can be rated of central concern to the average educated Englishman. All the same, there are sections of this difficult book which discuss very ordinary matters, such as the odd systems we use in naming our pets and our garden roses. But the four-year gap between the publication of the French and the English editions is an index of the problems of translation. The present English version (*The Savage Mind*) is the work of several hands. The text has the approval of Lévi-Strauss himself but has been described by an American critic as "execrable," and the translator who was originally commissioned by the English publishers has repudiated all responsibility. Trouble starts even with the title. The obvious translation of *La Pensée sauvage* would have been *Savage Thought*, a version supported by the somewhat baffling dust jacket of the original French edition, which displayed an illustration of wild pansies, purposely recalling Shakespeare's "there is pansies, that's for thoughts." *The Savage Mind* drags us back to *l'esprit humain*—the human mind—which, as we have seen, is hard to rescue from the metaphysical implications of Hegel's *Geist* or Durkheim's collective consciousness. But, in fact, *La Pensée sauvage* is not really concerned with metaphysics at all; it is about logic.

The fundamental theme is that we are at fault if we follow Lévy-Bruhl (and by derivation Sartre) in thinking that there is a historical contrast between the "prelogical" mentality of primitives and the "logical" mentality of modern man. Primitive people are no more mystical in their approach to reality than we are. The distinction rather is between a logic which is constructed out of observed contrasts in the sensory qualities of concrete objects—e.g., the difference between raw and cooked, wet and dry, male and female—and a logic which depends upon the formal contrasts of entirely abstract entities—e.g., plus and minus or $\log_e x$ and $x^e$. The latter kind of logic, which even in our own society is used only by highly specialized experts, is a different way of talking about the same kind of thing. Primitive thought differs from scientific thought much as the use of an abacus differs from mental arithmetic, but the fact that, in our present age, we are coming to depend on things outside ourselves—such as computers—to help us with our problems of communication and calculation makes this an appropriate moment to examine how primitive peoples likewise are able to make sense of the events of daily life by reference to codes composed of things outside themselves—such as the attributes of animal species.

As an indication of just how complicated this "logic of the concrete" is supposed to be, I give below a quotation from *Mythologiques* II which ties in an argument about categories of musical instruments with an argument about categories of food, modes of food preparation, and types of container. In this particular example all the ethnographic evidence is drawn from the cultural context of South American Indians, but Lévi-Strauss maintains that much the same permutations and combinations will hold good everywhere. The passage quoted assumes that we are already familiar with the general frame of discourse which has been developed in *Mythologiques* I and the earlier parts of *Mythologiques* II. One aspect of this may be illustrated by going back to my prime example about traffic lights (pages 17*ff*.) and then turning to the Table at page 49. In the latter, the "systems" of garments, food, furniture, etc. can be subjected to permutation just as are my three colors. So too with types of sound. With light signals we can convey messages by varying the frequency and duration of the light flashes, changing the colors, and so on, but the most basic distinction is simply to turn the lights on and off. So too with dress, the most radical distinction is naked/clothed; with music, it is noise/silence.

Hence it emerges that in the pages of *Mythologiques* certain basic oppositions are constantly being reiterated and combined into patterns. These include not only the paired dimensions incorporated in the Culinary Triangle (pages 25–28) and the schema of Figure 5 (page 76) but also a number of others, notably light/darkness, noise/silence, naked/clothed, sacred/profane.

A newcomer is bound to feel very puzzled as to why such a seemingly random set of dichotomies should be felt to cohere together to form a single macro-set, and it is a measure of Lévi-Strauss' intellectual achievement that he is able to establish a fairly convincing case for holding that this is so. Without prejudging that larger issue I can at least illustrate part of such a total "system" from a well-known example.

In classical mythology thunder (noise) expresses the anger of Zeus (sacred), whose drink is nectar, a distillation of (fresh) flowers (nature). Incidentally it seems to be generally true that, in the language of ancient and primitive mythologies, which did not need to cope with the cacophony of our industrial age, loud noises are always an attribute of the divine. Readers who find this implausible should remember that even in Christian eschatology the end of everything, which is also the day of judgment, will be announced by a trumpet call; and that until quite recent times church bells were much the loudest noise that ordinary individuals ever had to endure.

But let me get back to my promised example of the logic of the concrete. In *Mythologiques II* the themes of honey and tobacco are seen as the "penumbra of cooking" (*les entours de la cuisine*) and their contrasts are said to correspond, in the logic of mythology, to contrasts "internal to the category of noise" such as the oppositions continuous sound *vs.* discontinuous sound or modulated sound *vs.* unmodulated sound. The argument is that objects and the sensory characteristics of

hings "out there" are manipulated by the brain, through
the thought system incorporated in myth, just as if they
were symbols in a mathematical equation.

> When used as a ritual rattle [*hochet*] the calabash is
> an instrument of sacred music, utilized in conjunc-
> tion with tobacco which the myths conceive under
> the form of [an item of] culture included within
> nature; but when used to hold water and food, the
> calabash is an instrument of profane cooking, a con-
> tainer destined to receive natural products, and thus
> appropriate as an illustration of the inclusion of
> nature within culture. And it is the same for the
> hollow tree which, as a drum, is an instrument of
> music whose summoning role is primarily social, and
> which when holding honey, has to do with nature if
> it is a question of fresh honey being enclosed within
> its interior, and with culture if it is a question of
> honey being put to ferment within the trunk of a tree
> which is not hollow by nature but hollowed artificially
> to make it into a trough. (*Mythologiques II*, pp.
> 406–407)

If Lévi-Strauss is justified in believing that primitive
people think like that, then quite clearly the Frazer–
Lévy-Bruhl–Sartre notion that primitive thought is
characterized by naïveté, childishness, superstition,
and so on, is wholly misplaced. Lévi-Strauss' primitives
are just as sophisticated as we are; it is simply that
they use a different system of notation.

But is he justified? The skeptics have no difficulty in
finding points for criticism. The ethnographic worry is
that Lévi-Strauss may have unconsciously selected his
evidence so as to fit his theory, very much as Frazer
used to do. His evidence *illustrates* his theory, but suppose he had chosen other evidence: might not the whole
argument fall to pieces? At this stage in the demonstra-

tion, he had already made reference to three hundred and fifty-three different myths, but there is a great deal of other, rather similar stuff which he might have used, and we have to take it on trust that it really all says the same thing. In actual fact, despite the convolutions and complexity, I think this particular case does stand up, but the fault, if there is one, is that Lévi-Strauss tries to make his mathematics of manipulated sensory objects too systematic. He fails to allow for the fact that whereas the symbols used by mathematicians are emotionally neutral—$ix$ is not more *exciting* than $x$ just because $i$ is an imaginary number—the concrete symbols used in primitive thought are heavily loaded with taboo valuations. Consequently, psychological factors such as evasion and repression tend to confuse the logical symmetries. This does not mean that Lévi-Strauss' calculus must be invalid, but it may be much less precise than he seems to suggest. Or to put the same point another way: because he takes his cue from Jakobson-style linguistic theory and the mechanics of digital computers, Lévi-Strauss tends to imply—as is clearly shown in the passage cited above—that the whole structure of primitive thought is binary. Now there is not the slightest doubt that the human brain does have a tendency to operate with binary counters in all sorts of situations—but it can operate in other ways as well. A fully satisfactory mechanical model of the human mind would certainly contain many analogue features which do *not* occur in digital computers. So far, the Lévi-Straussian scheme of analysis has not taken this into account.

Even so, novices who tackle *La Pensée sauvage* as their introduction to the mind of Lévi-Strauss will, if they are patient, get an enormous brain-twisting enjoyment out of the first eight chapters. True, they will not be in a position to judge whether Lévi-Strauss is correct in claiming that his mythologic is a universal human characteristic, but they will certainly begin to see some of their own familiar behavior in a new light. I would commend in particular the extensive discussion of our conventions concerning the names we give to animals which forms part of the chapter entitled "The Individual as a Species." The basic point here is that, with us, dogs, as pets, are a part of human society but not quite human, and this is expressed when we give them names which are like human names but nearly always slightly different (or so Lévi-Strauss insists). On the other hand, when we give nicknames to birds—e.g., Jenny Wren, Tom Tit, Jack Daw, Robin Redbreast—they are normal human names. The difference is that the "nonhuman" names of pet dogs are names of individuals, whereas the "human" names of birds are applied indiscriminately to any member of a whole species. This is the distinction between metonymic and metaphoric modes of symbolic association:

Birds are given human Christian names in accordance with the species to which they belong more easily than are other zoological classes, because they can be permitted to resemble men for the very reason that they are so different. They are feathered, winged, oviparous and they are also physically separated from human society by the element in which it is their privilege to move. As a result of this fact, they form a community which is independent of our own but, precisely because of this independence, appears to us like another society, homologous to that in which we live: birds love freedom; they build themselves homes in which they live a family life and nurture their young; they often engage in social relations with other members of their species; and they communicate with them by acoustic means recalling articulated language.

Consequently everything objective conspires to make us think of the bird world as a metaphorical human society: is it not after all literally parallel to it on another level? There are countless examples in mythology and folklore to indicate the frequency of this mode of representation.

The position is exactly the reverse in the case of dogs. Not only do they not form an independent society; as "domestic" animals they are part of human society, although with so low a place in it that we should not dream of . . . designating them in the same way as human beings. . . . On the contrary, we allot them a special series: "Azor," "Médor," "Sultan," "Fido," "Diane" (the last of these is of course a human christian name but in the first instance conceived as mythological). Nearly all these are like stage names, forming a series parallel to the names people bear in ordinary life or, in other words, metaphorical names. Consequently when the relation between (human and animal) species is socially conceived as metaphorical, the relation between the respective systems of naming takes on a metonymical character; and when the relation between species is conceived as metonymical, the system of naming assumes a metaphorical character. (*The Savage Mind*, pp. 204, 205)

The catch, of course, as any pet-loving Englishman or American will immediately recognize, is that these broad French generalizations do *not* hold up as soon as one crosses the Straits of Dover! A great many English dogs have names *identical* with those of their human friends. Be that as it may, Lévi-Strauss then goes on to make further learned generalizations about the names French farmers give their cows:

Now the names given to cattle belong to a different
series from birds' or dogs'. They are generally de-
scriptive terms referring to the color of their coats,
their bearing or temperament: "Rustaud," "Russet,"
"Blanchette," "Douce," etc.; these names have a metaphorical character but they differ from the names
given to dogs in that they are epithets coming from
the syntagmatic chain while the latter come from
the paradigmatic series; the former thus tend to
derive from speech, the latter from language. (*The
Savage Mind*, p. 206)

Here again, the Englishman is out of line, though he
does better when it comes to racehorses! The trouble is
that Lévi-Strauss always wants to force his evidence
into completely symmetrical molds:

If therefore birds are *metaphorical human beings* and
dogs *metonymical human beings*, cattle may be
thought of as *metonymical inhuman beings* and racehorses as *metaphorical inhuman beings*. Cattle are
contiguous only for want of similarity, racehorses
similar only for want of contiguity. Each of these two
categories offers the converse image of one of the two
other categories, which themselves stand in the relation of inverted symmetry. (*The Savage Mind*, p. 207)

But supposing the English evidence doesn't really fit?
Well, no matter, the English are an illogical lot of bar-
barians in any case.

Don't misunderstand me. *The Savage Mind* taken as
a whole is an entrancing book. The exploration of the
way we (primitives and civilized alike) use different
kinds of language for purposes of classification, and of
the way that the categories which relate to social (cultural) space are interwoven with the categories which
relate to natural space is packed with immensely stimu-
lating ideas. But you should not always believe what is
said! When, for example, Lévi-Strauss claims that the

names of racehorses have the quality they do have *because* racehorses "do not form part of human society either as subjects or objects. Rather, they constitute the desocialized condition of existence of a private society; that which lives off racecourses or frequents them" (*The Savage Mind*, p. 206)—the train of thought is fascinating, but what sort of truth is involved? Even if we grant that the names given to racehorses form a class which can be readily distinguished, is this juxtaposition of the type of name and the type of social context anything more than a debating trick? The question needs to be asked. Whether it can be fairly answered I am not sure. Each reader needs to consider the evidence and think it out for himself.

What will doubtless puzzle the novice—more particularly when he comes to *Mythologiques II*—is how on earth Lévi-Strauss comes upon his basic oppositions in the first place. How could it ever occur to anyone that an opposition between roast pork and boiled cabbage might reflect a fundamental characteristic of human thinking, or that honey and tobacco of all things might come to have a significance as fundamental as that which opposes rain and drought? The answer, I think, is that Lévi-Strauss starts at the other end. He first asks himself: how is it and why is it that men, who are a part of nature, manage to see themselves as other than nature even though, in order to subsist, they must constantly maintain relations with nature? He then observes, simply as a fact of archaeology rather than ethnography, that ever since the most remote antiquity men have employed fire to transform their food from a natural raw state to an artificial cooked state. Why is this? Men do not *have* to cook their food; they do so for symbolic reasons to show that they are men and not beasts. So fire and cooking are basic symbols by which

culture is distinguished from nature. But what about
the honey and tobacco? In the case of cooked food the
fire serves to convert the inedible natural product into
an edible cultural product; in the case of honey the fire
is used only to drive away the bees—that is, to separate
the food, which can be eaten raw, from its natural
surroundings; in the case of tobacco it is the conversion
of the food by fire into a nonsubstance—smoke—which
makes it a food. So here already we have a set of
counters of different shapes and sizes each with a front
and a back which can be fitted together into patterns
and which *could* be used to represent the exchanges
and transformations which take place in human relations, as when a *boy* becomes an *adult*, or the *sister* of
A becomes the *wife* of B. With some such framework of
possibilities in his mind, plus the basic proposition that
mythology is concerned to make statements about the
relations between man and nature and between man
and man, Lévi-Strauss looks at his evidence and the
pieces of the puzzle begin to fit together.

Because the game is unfamiliar the whole business at
first seems very astonishing; there must be a catch in
it somewhere. On the other hand, if Lévi-Strauss' basic
assumptions were valid it could hardly be otherwise. And
even if his argument eventually has to be repudiated in
certain details, we simply *must* accept certain fundamental parts of it. Any knowledge that the individual
has about the external world is derived from structured
messages which are received through the senses—
patterned sound through the ears, patterned light
through the eyes, patterned smell through the nose, and
so on. But since we are aware of a *single* total experience—*not* a sound world plus a sight world plus a
smell world—it must be because the coding of the
various sensory signal systems can be made consistent—

so that hearing *and* sight *and* smell *and* taste *and* touch, etc., seem all to be giving the *same* message. The problem then is simply to devise a means of breaking the code. Lévi-Strauss thinks he has solved this problem; even those who have doubts can hardly fail to be astonished by the ingenuity of the exercise.

The ninth chapter of *La Pensée sauvage* is of a different kind from the rest and I have already made some remarks about it (see pages 6–8). Here I will do no more than repeat that what Lévi-Strauss seems to be saying is that Sartre attaches much too much importance to the distinction between history, as a record of actual events which occurred in a recorded historical sequence, and myth, which simply reports that certain events occurred as in a dream, without special emphasis on chronological sequence. History records structural transformations diachronically over the centuries; ethnography records structural transformations synchronically across the continents. In either case the scientist, as observer, is able to record the possible permutations and combinations of an interrelated system of ideas and behaviors. The intelligibility of the diachronic transformations is no greater and no less than the intelligibility of the synchronic transformations. By implication, the only way to make sense of history would be to apply to it the method of myth analysis which Lévi-Strauss has exhibited in his study of American mythology. Whether such an argument could possibly have any appeal to professional historians or philosophers of history it is not for me to say. Certainly it lies far off the beaten track of conventional anthropology, which for nearly half a century has paid little attention either to grand philosophy or to speculative interpretations of the nature of history.

So let us go back to some conventional anthropology.

The Elementary Structures of Kinship

# vi

And so at last we come to Lévi-Strauss' contributions to kinship theory. This is technical anthropological stuff, and readers who prefer a diet of soufflé· to suet pudding must mind their digestion.

This part of Lévi-Strauss' work was mostly published before 1949. I have ignored the chronology because, in this area of study, I am quite out of sympathy with Lévi-Strauss' position, but I must now try to explain what the argument is all about. One long-established anthropological tradition, which goes back to the publication of Morgan's *Systems of Consanguinity and Affinity of the Human Family* (1871), is to attach especial importance to the way words are used to classify genealogically related individuals. Although there are thousands of different human languages, all kin-term systems belong to one or other of about half a dozen "types." How should we explain this? Lévi-Strauss does not follow Morgan at all closely, but he assumes, as we might expect, that any particular system of kin terms is a syntagm of the "system" of all possible systems, which is, in turn, a precipitate of a universal human psychology. This line of thought is consistent with the "formal ethnography" of Lounsbury and others in the United States,[1] but is quite incompatible with the position of most British functionalist anthropologists. If pressed, the latter will argue that the different major types of kin-term system are a response to different patterns of social organization rather than to any universal attribute of the human mind.

All the same, despite their contempt for kinship words, the functionalists attach great importance to the study of kinship behavior. There is no mystery about this. Anthropologists are usually observing human beings in situations where the facilities for transport and communication are, by modern standards, very bad. Most of the individuals under study spend their whole lives within a few miles of the locality in which they were born, and in such circumstances most neighbors are biological kin. This does not mean that the people concerned will always recognize one another as kin or that they must inevitably attach special value to ties of kinship, but they may do so, and the anthropologist's experience is that this is very likely.

The general background of kinship theory lies outside the scope of this book, but there is one key point which must be understood. When anthropologists talk about kinship they are concerned with social behaviors

[1] See H. W. Scheffler, "Structuralism in Anthropology," in Jacques Ehrmann, ed., *Structuralism*, a double issue of *Yale French Studies*, Nos. 36–37 (1966), pp. 75 ff.

and not biological facts, and the two sets of data are often so widely discrepant that it is often convenient to discuss kinship without any reference to biology. All the same, any action which is labeled "kinship behavior" must in the last analysis have some tenuous link with biology—it must trace back to the self-evident fact that a mother is "related" to her own child and that brothers and sisters (siblings) of the same mother are related to one another.

Most kinship facts present themselves to the field anthropologist in two ways. In the first place, as I have said, his informants use a kinship terminology—words such as father, mother, uncle, aunt, cousin, etc.—to sort out the people in their vicinity into significant groups; in the second place it emerges that there are various sets of behaviors and attitudes which are considered especially appropriate or inappropriate between any two individuals deemed to be related in a particular way—e.g., it may be said that a man should never speak in the presence of his mother-in-law or that it would be a good thing if he were to marry a girl who falls into the same kin-term class as his mother's brother's daughter.

If we are trying to understand the day-to-day behavior of people living in close face-to-face relationship, facts such as these are clearly of great significance, and a good deal of the field anthropologist's research time is taken up with discovering just how these two frames of reference—the system of verbal categories and the system of behavioral attitudes—are interconnected. But for the chair-borne anthropologist, whether he be an inexperienced student or a senior professor, the data of kinship offer delights of quite another kind.

In its original context a kinship terminology is just a part of a spoken language; nothing particular separates kinship words from other words—indeed most kinship words have non-kinship meanings. Here are two examples: If you address someone as "Father O'Brien" you probably believe that he is both celibate and childless, and in the English East Anglian dialect the word "mother" used to mean an unmarried girl! However, if we ignore context and rely exclusively on orthodox dictionary definitions the words of any kinship vocabulary can be treated as a closed set—the elements of an algebraic matrix which refers exclusively to genealogical connections. Once the words have been isolated in this way the investigator is tempted to believe that this set of terms is logically coherent, and that other sets of terms, derived in a similar way from other languages, must have a comparable coherence. In this way the analysis of kinship terminologies becomes an end in itself, to which the original facts on the ground are related only as a tiresome and perhaps misleading irrelevance.

In his earlier papers, Lévi-Strauss displayed a healthy skepticism about this sort of thing, but as his own field experience recedes further into the background he has become more and more obsessed with his search for universals applicable to all humanity, and increasingly contemptuous of the ethnographic evidence. In a recent paper he has remarked, with regard to the analysis of kinship terminologies:

> F. G. Lounsbury and I. R. Buchler have proved that these nomenclatures manifest a kind of logical perfection which makes them authentic objects of scientific study; this approach has also permitted Lounsbury to expose the unreliability of some of the documentary material we are accustomed to handling without ever questioning its value. ("The Future of Kinship Studies," p. 13)

My disagreement here is basic. Lévi-Strauss has said somewhere that he considers that social anthropology is a "branch of semiology," which would imply that its central concern is with the internal logical structure of the meanings of sets of symbols. But for me the real subject matter of social anthropology always remains the actual social behavior of human beings. Whether or not kinship nomenclatures can be regarded as "authentic objects of scientific research" is perhaps a matter for debate, but most emphatically the logical analysis of these term systems cannot be used to determine whether any particular body of documentary material is or is not "reliable."

Anyway, despite these later tendencies, Lévi-Strauss' main contribution to kinship theory has not been concerned with the trivialities of kin-term logic but with the structure of conventional rules of marriage. This work is of interest to all anthropologists even though its details are open to the same kind of objection as before—namely, that Lévi-Strauss is liable to become so fascinated by the logical perfection of the "systems" he is describing that he disregards the empirical facts.

The orthodox tradition of functional anthropology is to start any discussion of kinship behavior with a reference to the elementary family. A child is related to both its parents by ties of filiation and to its brothers and sisters by ties of siblingship. These links provide the basic bricks out of which kinship systems are built up. Other discriminations depend on whether or not either parent has children by another spouse, whether or not affinal kinship (established by marriage) is or is not treated as "the same" as kinship based in filiation and siblingship, and so on.[2]

[2] A. R. Radcliffe-Brown, *Structure and Function in Primitive Society* (Glencoe, Ill., 1952), p. 51.

Lévi-Strauss puts the emphasis elsewhere. Admittedly, in the vast majority of societies, a child needs to have two recognized parents before it can be accepted as a fully legitimate member of society, but the legitimacy of the child depends upon the relationship between the parents rather than the relationship between the parents and the child. So Lévi-Strauss would claim that the conventional analysis starts at the wrong place.

The average young adult is a member of a group of siblings (A) and, as a consequence of marriage, will be brought into a new (affinal) kind of relationship with another group of siblings (B). (See Fig. 6) The relation-

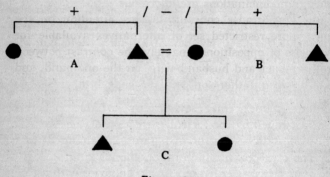

*Figure 6*

ship of siblingship and the the relationship of affinity are thus structurally contrasted as: $+/-$. As a result of the marriage, a third group of siblings (C) will be generated, and this new group will be related to each of the previous groups, but *how* it will be related will depend on a variety of circumstances. All that one can say at this stage is that *if the system is one of unilineal descent, either patrilineal (C→A) or matrilineal (C→B)* then the *relationships between members of A and members of C must in some sense be the "opposite of the relationships between members of B and the members of C.*

A complete analysis of this superficially simple situation would require consideration of a wide variety of "types" of relationship—e.g., brother/brother, brother/sister, husband/wife, father/son, father/daughter, mother/son, mother/daughter, mother's brother/sister's son, mother's sister/sister's son, mother's brother/sister's daughter, mother's sister/sister's daughter, father's sister/brother's son, father's brother/brother's son, father's sister/brother's daughter, father's brother/brother's daughter—and already the possible permutations and combinations are enormous.

But Lévi-Strauss concentrates his attention on the much more restricted set of alternatives available for two pairs of oppositions—namely, the contrast between brother/sister and husband/wife, on the one hand, and that between father/son and mother's brother/sister's son on the other. Let us represent the alternatives offered by the first opposition (X) by the words "mutuality" (+) and "separation" (−), and the alternatives offered by the second opposition (Y) by the words "familiarity" (+) and "respect" (−). Then we can draw up a matrix of possibilities of the same kind as that discussed on page 20. Thus in Figure 7, +/− in Column X stands for "mutuality/separation," but +/− in Column Y stands for "familiarity/respect."

According to Lévi-Strauss' rather one-sided reading of the ethnographic evidence all four possible combinations actually occur, and he claims, on grounds which do not seem very substantial, that this total system of possibilities is a human universal: "this structure is the most elementary form of kinship which can exist. It

| Principle of Descent | (Tribal Group) | X | | Y | |
|---|---|---|---|---|---|
| | | brother/ sister | : hus-band/ wife | father/ : son | mother's brother/ sister's son |
| MATRI-LINEAL | Trobriand | − | + | + | − |
| | Siuai | + | − | + | − |
| | Dobu | + | − | + | − |
| PATRI-LINEAL | Kubutu | + | − | + | − |
| | Cherkess | + | − | − | + |
| | Tonga | − | + | − | + |

*Figure* 7

is properly speaking the *unit of kinship*," and he then goes on to say that "in order for a kinship structure to exist, three types of family relations must always be present: a relation of consanguinity, a relation of affinity and a relation of descent."

In my view, this argument is fallacious for a variety of reasons, the most important being that Lévi-Strauss here confuses the notion of *descent*, a legal principle governing the transmission of rights from generation to generation, with the notion of *filiation*, the kinship link between parent and child. It is the same kind of confusion which leads him to suppose that the incest taboo is simply the converse of exogamy. Another point on which the argument appears vulnerable is that it is male-centered, but here Lévi-Strauss finds his justification in the ethnography. He claims that his point of departure, the transaction by which a sister changes her role to that of wife, is preferable to its inverse, the transaction by which a brother changes his role to that of husband, on empirical rather than logical grounds:

"In human society it is the men who exchange the women, and not *vice versa*." (*Structural Anthropology*, p. 47)

To the nonanthropologist all this must seem highly artificial, but for Lévi-Strauss it is a step in the direction of making the study of apparently freakish custom a problem for *scientific* investigation; or, to put it differently, it represents the establishment of a generalization from diverse particulars.

In the history of anthropology the empirical facts emerged the other way round. Lowie, in his early textbook *Primitive Society*, gives a long series of examples of the "avunculate," a term which he applies somewhat indiscriminately to almost any special relationship linking a mother's brother with his sister's son.[3] That such special relationships existed in apparently random world-wide distribution has been known to ethnographers for nearly a hundred years and the most diverse explanations have been offered to account for such customs. Some of these explanations seem to fit very well with particular sets of *local* facts,[4] but the apparent merit of Lévi-Strauss' approach is that he offers a *general* theory which should apply wherever there is any ideology of unilineal descent.

Unfortunately, we must at once draw a caveat. As may be seen from Figure 7, Lévi-Strauss originally offered six positive examples to illustrate his thesis, but he never considers the possibility of negative cases which do not fit his logical schema. Moreover, the argument, as presented, presumes that unilineal descent

---

[3] R. H. Lowie, *Primitive Society* (New York, 1920), p. 78.
[4] See Radcliffe-Brown, *Structure and Function in Primitive Society*, Chapter 1; and J. Goody, "The Mother's Brother and the Sister's Son in West Africa." *Journal of the Royal Anthropological Institute*, No. 89 (1959), pp. 61–88.

systems are universal, which is wholly untrue, and, because it is untrue, Lévi-Strauss' final grandiose flourish —"the avuncular relationship, in its most general form, is nothing but a corollary, now covert, now explicit, of the universality of the incest taboo" (*Structural Anthropology*, p. 51)—seems to be reduced to nonsense.

However that may be, Lévi-Strauss' major kinship treatise, *Les Structures élémentaires de la parenté* (1949) is no more than an enormously elaborated and convoluted version of this general proposition, and it suffers throughout from the same defects. Logical arguments are *illustrated* by means of allegedly appropriate ethnographic evidence, but no attention whatever is paid to the negative instances which seem to abound.

The big book starts off with a very old-fashioned review of "the incest problem" which brushes aside the substantial evidence that there have been numerous historical societies in which "normal" incest taboos did not prevail. This allows Lévi-Strauss to follow Freud in declaring that the incest taboo is the cornerstone of human society. His own explanation of this allegedly universal natural law depends upon a theory of social Darwinism similar to that favored by the English nineteenth-century anthropologist Edward Tylor. The latter maintained that, in the course of evolution, human societies had the choice of giving their womenfolk away to create political alliances or of keeping their womenfolk to themselves and getting killed off by their numerically superior enemies. In such circumstances, natural selection would operate in favor of societies enforcing rules of exogamy, which Tylor equated with the converse of the incest taboo. So also does Lévi-Strauss. The error is rudimentary: "The distinction between incest and exogamy . . . is really only the difference between sex and marriage, and while every teenager knows the difference many anthropologists get them confused."[5] The fact is that in all human societies of which we have detailed knowledge, the conventions governing sex relations are quite different from the conventions governing marriage, so there is no case for saying that in the beginning the latter must have been derived from the former.

Once past this initial hurdle, Lévi-Strauss goes on to discuss the logical possibilities of systems of exchange and then to consider certain rather specialized forms of marriage regulation as examples of these logical possibilities.

The argument about exchange, as such, is pretty much in line with Mauss' *Essai sur le don* (1924) and with the views of the British functionalists (for example, Firth). The conventions of gift-giving are interpreted as symbolic expressions of something more abstract, the network of relationships which links together members of the society in question. The giving of women in marriage and the consequent forging of a special form of artificial kinship—that is to say, the creation of the relationship between brothers-in-law— is seen as simply a special case, an extension in the converse direction of the process whereby gifts of food are habitually exchanged on ceremonial occasions to express the rights and obligations of existing ties of kinship and affinity. In the jargon of Barthes' semiology, "gift exchange" constitutes a "system," a general language code for the expression of relationships. "Exchange of women" is one system within that "system"; "exchange of valuables other than women" is another. The routine sequence of exchanges which occurs in the context of a particular marriage in a particular society

[5] R. Fox, *Kinship and Marriage* (London, 1967), p. 54.

is a syntagm of the "system." The methodology for breaking the code is the same as that which has been described in earlier chapters. The marriage systems of different societies are treated as paradigmatic transformations of an underlying common logical structure. However, Lévi-Strauss does not regard marriage (i.e., the exchange of women between men) as just one alternative system of exchange among many; it is primary. He claims that because, in the case of women, the relationship symbolized by the exchange is also constituted by the thing exchanged, the relationship and its symbol are one and the same, and the giving of women in marriage must be considered the most elementary of all forms of exchange. It must be deemed to have preceded (in evolution) the exchange of goods, where the sign and the relationship that is signified are distinct.

As with the case of the earlier avunculate argument, Lévi-Strauss' discussion of marriage rules in *Les Structures élémentaires de la parenté* (1949) was distorted by his erroneous belief that the great majority of primitive societies have systems of unilineal descent. By now he has come to realize that this was a mistake, and there is an interesting contrast between pages 135–36 of the first edition and pages 123–24 of its 1967 successor. In the latter he weakly concludes: "Nevertheless, since this book is limited to a consideration of elementary structures, we consider it is justifiable to leave provisionally on one side examples which relate to undifferentiated filiation." [!] Incidentally, as time goes on, it becomes increasingly difficult to understand just what Lévi-Strauss really means by "elementary structures." The reader needs to appreciate that the great majority of what are usually considered to be "ultraprimitive" societies (*e.g.*, Congo Pygmies and Kalahari Bushmen) do *not* have systems of unilineal descent.

However, let me try to expound Lévi-Strauss' thesis. First let us consider Figure 8 as an elaborated form of Figure 6 (page 110) in which two unilineal descent groups are represented as three generations of sibling pairs: A1, A2, A3 on the one hand, and B1, B2, B3 on the other. Let us suppose that A1 and B1 are allied by marriage, either because the A1 male is married to the B1 female or vice versa, or because both of these marriages have taken place. Then, in the jargon of anthropology, the B2 siblings are classificatory first cross-cousins of the A2 siblings, while the B3 siblings are classificatory second cross-cousins[6] of the A3 siblings. Lévi-Strauss first of all considers various kinds of hypothetical marriage conventions which would have the effect of perpetuating an alliance between the A group and the B group once it had been established.

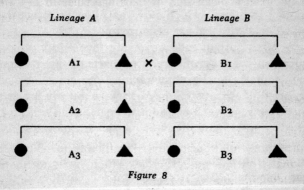

Figure 8

---

[6] A cross-cousin is a cousin of the type "mother's brother's child" or "father's sister's child" as distinct from a parallel cousin, who is a cousin of the type "mother's sister's child" or "father's brother's child."

If, for example, the exchange were directly reciprocal, so that the A males always exchanged sisters with the B males, this would be the equivalent of a marriage rule expressing preference for marriage with a mother's brother's daughter or a father's sister's daughter. But a different kind of over-all political structure would result if the rules required an exchange of sisters with a second cousin, so that, for example, a man marries his mother's mother's brother's daughter's daughter or his mother's father's sister's daughter's daughter.

As a further complication he suggests that very simple organizations of this kind can be usefully distinguished as "harmonic" or "disharmonic." He recognizes only two types of descent—patrilineal and matrilineal—and two types of residence—virilocal and uxorilocal. (In anthropological jargon a virilocal residence rule requires a wife to join her husband on marriage, an uxorilocal rule requires a husband to join his wife.) Systems which are patrilineal-virilocal or matrilineal-uxorilocal are harmonic; systems which are patrilineal-uxorilocal or matrilineal-virilocal are disharmonic.

All these arguments are highly theoretical. By some stretching of the evidence some parts of the discussion can be illustrated by ethnographic facts which have been reported of the Australian Aborigines, but the latter are in no sense typical of primitive societies in other parts of the world, and there is no justification for Lévi-Strauss' apparent postulate that once upon a time all ultraprimitive human societies operated in accordance with an Australian structural model. On the contrary, there are good grounds for supposing that they did not.

However, for what it is worth, Lévi-Strauss maintains, on logical grounds, that harmonic structures are unstable and that disharmonic structures are stable, so that systems of the first type will tend to evolve into the second type, rather than *vice versa*, or alternatively that harmonic systems of "restricted exchange" provide the base from which have emerged harmonic systems of "generalized exchange." These terms need further explanation.

Lévi-Strauss classes all varieties of directly reciprocal sister exchange as falling into one major category *échange restreint* (restricted exchange) which he distinguishes from his other major category *échange généralisé* (generalized exchange). In restricted exchange, so the argument goes, a man gives away a sister only if he has a positive assurance that he will get back a wife; in generalized exchange he gives away his sister to one group but gambles that he will be able to get back a wife from some other group. The political alliance is widened—the individual gets two brothers-in-law where previously he had only one—but the risks are greater. Asymmetrical arrangements of this kind are equivalent to marriage rules in which marriage with one cross-cousin is approved and marriage with the other forbidden, *e.g.*:

| | |
|---|---|
| mother's brother's daughter approved but father's sister's daughter forbidden | "matrilateral cross-cousin marriage rule" |
| father's sister's daughter approved but mother's brother's daughter forbidden | "patrilateral cross-cousin marriage rule" |

Rules of the second kind have just the same practical consequence as rules based on a reciprocal exchange of sisters, so they are of no serious interest, though Lévi-

Strauss devotes much attention to their alleged occurrence and they have been the source of much anthropological argument. Rules of the first type ("matrilateral cross-cousin marriage") are much more common, and though Lévi-Strauss was by no means the first person to bring them into serious discussion, he did manage to make a number of theoretical observations which proved to be of considerable practical significance.

A matrilateral cross-cousin marriage rule, if it were strictly enforced, would produce a chain of lineages in a permanent affinal alliance of wife givers and wife receivers (Figure 9).

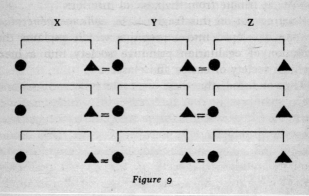

*Figure* 9

Such diagrams seem to contain a paradox: where will the men of Group Z get their wives? Where will the sisters of the men of Group X find their husbands? Lévi-Strauss discusses this puzzle at enormous length. Any summary of the argument, let alone of the rival arguments produced by other authors, would be preposterously misleading, but perhaps the heart of the matter is this: the system illustrated in Figure 9, as it works out in practice, must be in some sense circular.

Either the X group give their sisters to the Z group direct, or else through several intermediary groups of similar kind: in any event the women whom the Zs take in as wives are the equivalents of the women whom the Xs give away as sisters.

Lévi-Strauss recognizes that the difficulties in the way of maintaining such a system of "circulating connubium" for any length of time must be very considerable, and he claims that, in practice, the marriage circles will always break down into hierarchies such that the intermarrying lineages will be of different status. The resulting marriage system would then be hypergamous, with the groups at the top receiving women as tribute from their social inferiors.

Starting out on this fragile base, *échange généralisé* is then developed into a principle which explains the evolution of egalitarian primitive society into a hierarchical society of castes and classes.

Thus reduced, the theory sounds preposterous, and even when presented at full length it is still open to all kinds of criticism of the most destructive sort, and yet there *is* an odd kind of fit between some parts of the theory and some of the facts on the ground, even though, at times, the facts on the ground perversely turn Lévi-Strauss' argument back to front! For example, the systems in which hypergamous hierarchy is carried to the wildest extremes are associated with dowry rather than bride-price, while the systems in which matrilateral cross-cousin marriage is the rule mostly take the form in which the wife givers rank higher than the wife receivers.[7]

---

[7] In the 1967 and 1969 editions of his book Lévi-Strauss attempted to mask the fact that he had ever made this ethnographic error but the resulting patchwork in his text only leads to inconsistency. See Leach (1969).

Lévi-Strauss himself seems inclined to argue that if there are *any* ethnographic facts which are consistent with his general theory, then this alone is sufficient to prove that, in its basic essentials, the general theory is right, but even his most devoted followers could hardly accept that kind of proposition.

Elsewhere Lévi-Strauss has claimed that the superiority of his method is demonstrated by the fact that a vast multiplicity of types and subtypes of human society is here reduced to "a few basic and meaningful principles" (*Mythologiques I*, p. 127), but he fails to point out that the vast majority of human societies are not covered by his basic and meaningful principles at all! Moreover, there seems to be a major fallacy at the very root of his argument. According to Lévi-Strauss we need to think of

> marriage rules and kinship systems as a sort of language that is to say a set of operations designed to insure, between individuals and groups, a certain type of communication. The fact that the "message" would here be constituted by the *women of the group* who *circulate* between clans, lineages or families (and not, as in the case of language itself, by the *words of the group* circulating between individuals) in no way alters the fact that the phenomenon considered in the two cases is identically the same. (*Anthropologie structurale*, p. 69; cf. *Structural Anthropology*, p. 61, where a different and much less literal translation is offered)

But of course, there is no such identity. If I give an object into the possession of someone else, I no longer possess it myself. Possibly I shall gain something else in exchange and possibly I retain some residual claim on the original object, but I have limited my previous rights. If, on the other hand, I transmit a message to someone else by making a speech utterance, I do *not* deprive myself of anything at all; having shared my information with one listener I can repeat the operation and share it with another.

Certainly there is *some* kind of analogy between the two frames of reference—a collectivity of lineages which intermarry forms a "kinship community" in a sense which is, up to a point, comparable with the "speech community" formed by any collectivity of individuals who habitually converse with one another. But, as Lévi-Strauss himself has pointed out in a different context, the concept of *mutuality*—of sharing common resources—is in important respects diametrically opposed to the concept of *reciprocity*—the exchange of distinct but equivalent resources. (*Structural Anthropology*, p. 49)

However, irrespective of the merits of the particular case, the reader should note that Lévi-Strauss' over-all procedure for the analyses of marriage alliances is just the same as that which we have discussed elsewhere in the context of myth and totemism and the categories of cooking. He treats the possible preferences for marriage with a cousin of such and such a category as forming a set of logical alternatives, adherence to which will result in different over-all patterns of social solidarity within the total society. These different kinship systems, superimposed, constitute a set of paradigms (in the sense discussed on pages 48–50) which are manifested (*a*) in sets of kinship terms and (*b*) in institutions of marriage and exchange. Taken all together the paradigms will provide us with clues as to the internalized structural logic of the human mind.

The argument is systematic: first we consider societies with two intermarrying groups, then four, then eight, then a sequence of more complex asymmetrical types. It is all so elegantly done that even the most skeptical professional may find some difficulty in detecting the precise point at which the argument runs off at a tangent. In my view the end product is in large measure fallacious, but even the study of fallacies can prove rewarding.

Machines for the Suppression of Time

# vii

Let us go back to the beginning and try to pull the argument together. Lévi-Strauss' quest is to establish facts which are universally true of the "human mind" (*esprit humain*). What is universally true must be natural, but this is paradoxical because he starts out with the assumption that what distinguishes the human being from the man-animal is the distinction between culture and nature—i.e., that the humanity of man is that which is non-natural. Again and again in Lévi-Strauss' writings we keep coming back to this point: the problem is not merely "in what way is culture (as an attribute of humanity) distinguishable from nature (as an attribute of man)?" but also "in what way is the culture of *Homo sapiens* inseparable from the nature of humanity?"

Lévi-Strauss takes over from Freud the idea

that it is meaningful to talk about human beings' having an Unconscious as well as a Consciousness; and, for Lévi-Strauss as for Freud, the unconscious Id is natural, the conscious Ego is cultural. When Lévi-Strauss tries to reach into the "human mind" he is grasping at the structural aspects of the Unconscious. But Lévi-Strauss' approach is through linguistics rather than through psychology. The linguistic model which Lévi-Strauss employs is now largely out of date. Present-day theoreticians in the field of structural linguistics have come to recognize that the deep-level process of pattern generation and pattern recognition that is entailed by the human capacity to attach complex semantic significance to speech utterances must depend on mechanisms of much greater complexity than is suggested by the digital computer model which underlies the Jakobson–Lévi-Strauss theories. Jakobson's schema of a limited set of binary distinctive features common to all human languages is not necessarily false, but it is certainly inadequate. Where speech is concerned, the ultimate objective of research is to discover not merely how children learn to distinguish noise contrasts as significant but how they acquire the generative rules which allow them to distinguish meaningful patterns of sound in the first place and what sort of rules these may be. By comparison, the patterning of manifest cultural data with which Lévi-Strauss is playing is superficial. I am ready to concede that the structures which he displays are products of an unconscious mental process, but I can see no reason to believe that they are human universals. Bereft of Lévi-Strauss' resourceful special pleading they appear to be local, functionally determined attributes of particular individuals or of particular cultural groups (see above, pages 22–23). However, as Yvan Simonis has observed, although Lévi-Strauss originally set out to display the structure of the "human mind," he has ended up by telling us something about the structure of aesthetic perception.[1]

His starting point, let us remember, was that the specifically human quality of human beings is that they have a language. At one level this allows man to communicate and form social relations, and at another it is an essential element in the mysterious process we call "thinking," in that we must first categorize our environment and then represent these categories by symbols ("elements of language," "words") before we can "think" about them.

This process of "thinking" by means of word symbols (and other kinds of symbols) entails a highly complex interplay between the individual who is doing the thinking and the environment about which he is thinking. For example, in our culture an essential part of almost any intellectual operation is that the thinker should be able to externalize the words and numbers which are in his head and write them down on pieces of paper (or else make drawings and models of what he is thinking about). Thus considered, the operation "thinking about" consists of the manipulation of reduced models of ideas which started out in the first place as words, which symbolize "events" and "things" in the environment external to the thinker. Very recently, in the last decade or so, we have carried this externalization process a step further. Having created the "reduced model" in the form of a computer program, we can now design machines which do a great deal of the manipulation on their own account without any immediate feedback into the brain of the thinker at all.

[1] Yvan Simonis, *Claude Lévi-Strauss ou la "Passion de l'inceste"* (Paris, 1968).

In taking this step beyond ordinary verbal language and beyond ordinary written symbols to symbols which exist "out there" as part of the environment and which can, as it were, be made to play logical games by themselves without conscious human intervention, we seem to have almost gone full circle. Primitive man, before he had any writing, perhaps even before he had developed his spoken language to a point where it could be used as a refined instrument of logic, was already using things "out there" as instruments with which to think. This is the essence of Lévi-Strauss' arguments about totemic-species categories and food-preparation categories—they are categories which refer to things "out there" in the human environment and they are things good for thinking, not just things good to eat.

But, just as the reduced models of human thought which are "out there" can assume many different forms —e.g., the printed page of this book conveys information in quite a different way from either a length of computer tape or the grooves of a phonograph record—so also human thought which is *internal* to the individual brain can take on different forms. When we monitor our own speech we are thinking by means of patterned sound, but there are other ways also in which we treat sound patterns as "things good for thinking."

Completely random, mixed-up sound is just noise; it tells us nothing at all. But *patterned* sound of any kind will always convey information of some sort. Thus we can recognize the bark of a dog, the screech of an owl, or the noise of a passing motorcycle. Noises of these sorts are all patterned, though the patterning is of a different kind from that of a spoken language. It is not generated by our own unconscious mental processes. There is yet another class of patterned sounds, which we call music, which is neither speech in any

simple sense nor noise communicating information
about the outside world. For Lévi-Strauss, music is something of a test case. Music is of human, not animal,
origin; it is part of culture, not nature; yet it is not part
of a system of exchange in the same sense that spoken
language is a system of exchange; the meaning of music
cannot be reduced to a model or diagram in the way
that the meaning of a kinship system or a set of myths
may be reduced.

> But that music is a language by whose means mes-
> sages are elaborated, that such messages can be un-
> derstood by the many but sent out only by the few,
> and that it alone among all the languages unites the
> contradictory character of being at once intelligible
> and untranslatable—these facts make the creator of
> music a being like the gods and make music itself
> the supreme mystery of human knowledge. All other
> branches of knowledge stumble into it, it holds the
> key to their progress. (*Mythologiques I*, p. 26)

Yet myth and music (and dreaming) have certain
elements in common; they are, says Lévi-Strauss, "machines for the suppression of time" (*Mythologiques I*,
p.24); the last movement of a symphony is presupposed
by its beginning just as the end of a myth is already
implicit where it began. The repetitions and thematic
variations of a musical score produce responses in the
listener which depend in some way on his physiological
rhythms; and, in like measure (asserts Lévi-Strauss),
the repetitions and thematic variations of myth play
upon physiological characters of the human brain to
produce emotional as well as purely intellectual effects.
Furthermore, what the individual listener understands
when he hears a myth or a piece of music is in many
ways personal to himself; it is the *receiver* who decides

what the message is. In this respect myth and music are the converse of spoken language, where it is the *sender* who decides what the message is. The structural analysis of myth and of music will lead us to an understanding of the unconscious structure of "the human mind" because it is this unconscious (natural) aspect of the brain which is triggered into response by these special cultural (non-natural) devices:

> Myth and music thus appear as conductors of an orchestra of which the listeners are the silent performers. [*Le mythe et l'œuvre musicale apparaissent ainsi comme des chefs d'orchestre dont les auditeurs sont les silencieux exécutants.*] (*Mythologiques I*, pp. 25–26)

a remark which recalls Valéry's observation that poets should "reclaim from music their rightful heritage" (*reprendre à la musique leur bien*).[2]

The massive volumes of *Mythologiques* are designed to exhibit the logical mechanisms and concealed ambiguities which evoke these emotional responses, and the thesis is that when we really get down to the roots of the matter the interdependence of logical structure and emotional response is much the same everywhere—for the nature of man is everywhere the same.

Of course, there must be a sense in which Lévi-Strauss is right, and yet reductionism of this degree of comprehensiveness seems to defeat its own ends. When, in the early days of psychoanalysis, the orthodox Freudians asserted as dogma the universality of the Oedipus complex, the Oedipus complex as such became devoid of all

---

[2] *The Collected Works of Paul Valéry*, ed. J. Mathews, Vol. VII: *Paul Valéry: The Art of Poetry* (New York, 1958), p. 42.

analytical value. *All* evidence, no matter how contradictory it might appear, was forced into the predetermined mold. And the same kind of thing seems to be happening to Lévi-Strauss. His writings display an increasing tendency to assert *as dogma* that his discoveries relate to facts which are *universal* characteristics of the unconscious process of human thought. At first this was simply a matter of generalizing from his primary schema of binary oppositions and mediating middle terms (which is little more than the Hegelian triad of thesis, antithesis, synthesis), but lately the whole system seems to have developed into a self-fulfilling prophecy which is incapable of test because, by definition, it cannot be disproved. For example, a footnote to *Mythologiques III* reports on a private communication which the author had received from the distinguished Colombian ethnographer G. Reichel-Dolmatoff relating to a Chaco myth which uses wild honey as a metaphor for human sperm. Since the "philosophy of honey" which Lévi-Strauss has painfully extracted from the piled-up detail of *Mythologiques II* is "inspired by the analogy between this natural product and menstrual blood," one might have expected that Lévi-Strauss would be somewhat disconcerted, but the contrary is the case: "This remarkable inversion of a system which we have revealed as occurring in a vast territory stretching from Venezuela to Paraguay does not contradict our interpretation but enriches it by a supplementary dimension." (*Mythologiques III*, p. 340*n*.) But if "supplementary dimensions" can be added to meet every contrary case then the main theory can never be put to a critical test at all.

The genuinely valuable part of Lévi-Strauss' contribution, in my view, is not the formalistic search for binary oppositions and their multiple permutations and combinations but rather the truly poetic range of associations which he brings to bear in the course of his analysis: in Lévi-Strauss' hands complexity becomes revealing instead of confusing.

It is scarcely possible to give a demonstration of "revealing complexity" in a book this size, but anyone who wishes to pursue my comment further should take a look at the pages of *Le Pensée sauvage* where Lévi-Strauss gives a digest analysis of the myths and rituals associated by the Hidatsa Indians with their techniques of catching eagles. I have space here to quote only one paragraph: Lévi-Strauss is explaining why we can be confident that the mythical animal who first taught the Hidatsa to hunt eagles was not, as some reports have said, a bear but the wolverine (*carajou*). These Indians hunt eagles

by hiding in pits. The eagle is attracted by a bait placed on top and the hunter catches it with his bare hands as it perches to take the bait. And so the technique presents a kind of paradox. Man is the trap, but to play this part he has to go down into the pit, that is, to adopt the position of a trapped animal. He is both hunter and hunted at the same time. The wolverine is the only animal which knows how to deal with this contradictory situation: not only has it not the slightest fear of the traps set for it; it actually competes with the trapper by stealing his prey and sometimes even his traps. It follows . . . that the ritual importance of eagle hunting among the Hidatsa is at least partly due to the use of pits, to the assumption by the hunter of a particular *low* position (literally as we have just seen, figuratively as well) for capturing a quarry which is in the very *highest* position in an objective sense (eagles fly high) and also from a mythical point of view (the eagle being at the top of the mythical hierarchy of birds). (*The Savage Mind*, pp. 50–51)

All of which is surely very far removed from our own ways of thought? But are we sure about this? Notice, for example, that the Hidatsa triadic schema of Sky : Earth : Underworld : : Eagles : Bait : Man-Wolverine has exactly the same "structure" as the argument about colored traffic lights with which I started this discussion!

Taken as a whole, Lévi-Strauss' analysis shows us that, in the thinking of the Hidatsa, such practical economic matters as hunting and agriculture are inextricably entangled with attitudes toward cosmology, sanctity, food, women, life, and death, and certainly this is diametrically opposed to our own contemporary fashion which lays it down that, in order to rate as rational scientists, we must keep facts and values entirely separate. Our thinking is the product of a culture alienated from nature: that of the Hidatsa derives from a culture integrated with nature.

Yet even if we concede that, with us, there can be no room for poets in the laboratory, we ought to recognize that when we set such store by objective rationality there is loss as well as gain. The poetic experience carries its own (aesthetic) rewards. Hidatsa thinking on these matters had its counterpart in the ancient world. The underworld in which Ulysses sees and speaks with the departed heroes is no deeper than a ditch, while that to which Proserpina is annually abducted by Pluto has only the depth of a plough furrow: correspondingly the sky of the ancients was no higher than the tops of some very moderate hills. When Vico commented to this effect in the early eighteenth century he was imbued with admiration rather than contempt; it needed the arrogance of late-nineteenth-century materialism to reduce the poetry of primitive thought to the status of a childish superstition.

But if, as Lévi-Strauss seems to be saying, Vico's "poetic cosmography"[3] is a natural attribute of the "human mind," then it should lie somewhere within the hidden structures of our own collective unconscious. Perhaps even in the age of space rockets and hydrogen bombs Paradise need not be wholly beyond recall.

[3] See G. Vico, *The New Science of Giambattista Vico* (1744) (New York, 1961), p. 218.

SHORT BIBLIOGRAPHY

INDEX

# SHORT BIBLIOGRAPHY

The three most complete bibliographies of Lévi-Strauss' own writings and associated commentaries are given in Yvan Simonis, *Claude Lévi-Strauss ou la "Passion de l'inceste"* (Paris, 1968), pp. 357–70; M. Marc-Lipiansky, *Le Structuralisme de Lévi-Strauss* (Paris, 1973), pp. 326–32; and J. Pouillon and P. Maranda, eds., *Échanges et Communications* (2 vols., The Hague, 1970), pp. xv–xxiii.

A substantial proportion of Lévi-Strauss' writings are available in English, and in some cases the publication of the English text came first. The difference between the French and the English versions is often substantial. In his native language Lévi-Strauss is fond of playing tricks with words and inserting complex ambiguities in the form of puns. These verbal games greatly add to the reader's enjoyment and clearly constitute part of the message. In English translation most of these ambiguities disappear; the text becomes more lucid but it says less. For those who can read French easily I would always recommend the French version even when an author's English version exists.

Of Lévi-Strauss' principal works, only *La Vie familiale et sociale des Indiens Nambikwara* remains wholly untranslated. English versions of *Mythologiques I* and *II* have appeared, and the remaining volumes will presumably arrive later. The first English translation of *Tristes Tropiques*, carrying the French title in its American edition, lacks four chapters of the French original. The second English translation is complete. The 1949 edition of *Les Structures élémentaires de la parenté* was never translated into English; an English version of the revised 1967 edition was published in 1969, but it contains a special polemical attack against certain British social anthropologists who are said to have misinterpreted the structuralist gospel.

For the ordinary English or American reader the most sensible order in which to tackle Lévi-Strauss' writings would be to start with *Structural Anthropology*, which is a collection of key essays two of which, "Structural Analysis in Linguistics and Anthropology" and "The Structural Study of Myth" have been mentioned several times in the course of this book. The novice reader should then go on to read *Totemism* and *The Savage Mind*. Both these books are quite short and are closely related; they should be read at the same time. Addicts might then turn their attention to one of the full-length commentaries by French admirers. The two best to date are those by Simonis and Marc-Lipiansky.

## Works by Lévi-Strauss Cited in This Book

"L'analyse structurale en linguistique et en anthropologie," *Word: Journal of the Linguistic Circle of New York*, I, No. 2 (1945). An English version of this essay may be found in *Structural Anthropology*, Chapter 2.

*Anthropologie structurale*. Paris, 1958. English version, *Structural Anthropology*. New York, 1963.

"Contribution à l'étude de l'organisation sociale des Indiens Bororo," *Journal de la Société des Americanistes*, XXVIII, No. 2 (1936).

"The Future of Kinship Studies," Huxley Memorial Lecture, in *Proceedings of the Royal Anthropological Institute* (London, 1965).

"La Geste d'Asdiwal," *Annuaire de l'E.P.H.E.* (*Sciences Religieuses*) *1958–59* (Paris, 1960). An English version of this essay, "The Story of Asdiwal," may be found in E. R.

Leach, ed., *The Structural Study of Myth and Totemism*. London, 1967, pp. 1–48.

*Mythologiques I: Le cru et le cuit*. Paris. 1964. English version of Introduction in Jacques Ehrmann, ed., *Structuralism*, a double issue of *Yale French Studies*, Nos. 36–37 (October 1966), pp. 44–65. English version of entire book, translated by John and Doreen Weightman, *The Raw and the Cooked: Introduction to a Science of Mythology*, Vol. I. New York, 1969.

*Mythologiques II: Du miel aux cendres*. Paris, 1966. English version, translated by John and Doreen Weightman, *From Honey to Ashes*. New York, 1971.

*Mythologiques III: L'origine des manières de table*. Paris, 1968.

*Mythologiques IV: L'Homme nu*. Paris, 1972.

*La Pensée sauvage*. Paris, 1962. English version. *The Savage Mind*. Chicago, 1966.

*Race et Histoire*. Paris, 1952. English version, *Race and History*. New York, 1958.

"Réponses à quelques questions," *Esprit* (Paris, November, 1963), pp. 628–53.

"The Structural Study of Myth," *Journal of American Folklore*, Vol. 68, No. 270 (1955). A modified version of this essay may be found in *Structural Anthropology*, Chapter 11.

"La Structure et la forme. Réflexions sur un ouvrage de Vladimir Propp," *Cahiers de l'Institut des Sciences économiques appliquées* (Paris, 1960).

*Les Structures élémentaires de la parenté*. Paris, 1949. Rev. ed., 1967. English version of rev. ed., *Elementary Structures of Kinship*. Boston, 1969. ———

"Le Triangle culinaire," *L'Arc* (Aix-en-Provence), No. 26 (1965), pp. 19–29.

*Le Totémisme aujourd'hui*. Paris, 1962. English version, *Totemism*. Boston, 1962.

*Tristes Tropiques*. Paris, 1955. American version, translated by John Russell, omitting four chapters, *Tristes Tropiques*. New York, 1961. There is a new complete translation by John and Doreen Weightman, *Tristes Tropiques*. London, 1973.

*La Vie familiale et sociale des Indiens Nambikwara*. Paris, 1948.

## Works by Other Authors

There are now a number of English-language structuralist symposia which illustrate the variety of influence which Lévi-Strauss has exercised over his contemporaries. Those edited by Ehrmann, Lane, Maranda, and Robey deserve special note. Critical essays provoked by the publication of individual volumes of Lévi-Strauss' work are also very numerous. Among the most striking are those which have appeared in the pages of *The Times Literary Supplement* (February 29, 1965; September 2, 1968; February 7, 1972). It seems likely that the anonymous author of all three essays is George Steiner, who is a close personal friend of Lévi-Strauss (see his *Language and Silence* [1967], pp. 267–79). Octavio Paz' *Claude Lévi-Strauss: An Introduction* (London, 1970), has been commended by Lévi-Strauss himself, who has also expressed his approval of James A. Boon, *From Symbolism to Structuralism: Lévi-Strauss in a Literary Tradition* (Oxford, 1972). On the other hand, J. Piaget, *Structuralism* (London, 1971), deserves to be read because of its emphasis on forms of structuralism very different from those of Lévi-Strauss; in this regard see also Howard Gardner, *The Quest for Mind* (New York, 1973).

Bateson, G. *Naven*. New York, 1936.

Barthes, R. *The Elements of Semiology*. New York, 1968.

Chomsky, N. *Current Issues in Linguistic Theory*. The Hague, 1964.

———. *Syntactic Structures*. The Hague, 1964.

Davy, C. *Words in the Mind*. Cambridge, Mass., 1965.

Ehrmann, J., ed. *Structuralism*, a double issue of *Yale French Studies*, Nos. 36–37 (October, 1966). (Issued in paperback, New York, 1971.

Empson, W. *Seven Types of Ambiguity*. Cambridge, 1931.

Fox, R. *Kinship and Marriage*. London, 1967.

Frazer, J. G. *The Golden Bough* (abridged ed.). London, 1922.

Goldenweiser, A. "Totemism, an Analytical Study," *Journal of American Folklore*, XXIII (1910).

Goody, J. "The Mother's Brother and the Sister's Son in West Africa." *Journal of the Royal Anthropological Institute*, 89 (1959), pp. 61–88.

Hultkranz, A. *The North American Indian Orpheus Tradition*. New York, 1958.

Jakobson, R., and Halle, M. *Fundamentals of Language*. New York, 1956.

Lane, M. ed., *Structuralism: A Reader*. London, 1970.

Linch, E. "Kachin and Haka Chin: a Rejoinder to Lévi-Strauss." *Man* (NS) 4, pp. 277–285.

Lowie, R. H. *Primitive Society*. New York, 1920.

Maranda, P. and E. K., eds., *Structural Analysis of Oral Tradition*. Philadelphia, 1971.

Marc-Lipiansky, M. *Le Structuralisme de Lévi-Strauss*. Paris, 1973.

Mauss, M. "Essai sur le don," *L'Année sociologique* (2d series, 1923–24), 1924. English version, *The Gift*. London, 1954.

Morgan, L. P. *Systems of Consanguinity and Affinity of the Human Family*. Washington, D. C., 1871.

Pouillon, J. "Sartre et Lévi-Strauss, *L'Arc* (Aix-en-Provence), No. 26 (1965) pp. 55–60.

Pouillon, J. and Maranda, P. eds., *Echanges et Communications*, 2 vols. The Hague, 1970.

Radcliffe-Brown, A. R. "The Sociological Theory of Totemism," 1929. Reprinted as Chapter VI of Radcliffe-Brown, *Structure and Function in Primitive Society*. Glencoe, Ill., 1952.

———. "The Comparative Method in Social Anthropology," *Journal of the Royal Anthropological Institute*, 81 (1951), pp. 15–22.

———. *Structure and Function in Primitive Society*. Glencoe, Ill., 1952.

Ricoeur, P. "Structure et herméneutique," *Esprit* (Paris, November, 1963), pp. 596–627.

Robey, D. ed., *Structuralism: an Introduction*. Oxford, 1973.

Rose, H. J. *A Handbook of Greek Mythology*. New York, 1959.

Rousseau, J.-J. "Essai sur l'origine des langues." Geneva, 1783.

Sartre, J.-P. *Critique de la raison dialectique*. Paris, 1960.

Saussure, F. de. *Course in General Linguistics*. New York, 1959.

Scheffler, H. W. "Structuralism in Anthropology," in Jacques

Ehrmann, ed., *Structuralism*, a double issue of *Yale French Studies*, Nos. 36–37 (October, 1966), pp. 66–80.

Schniewind, J. "A Reply to Bultmann," in H. W. Bartsch, ed., *Kerygma and Myth*. London, 1953.

Simonis, Y. *Claude Lévi-Strauss ou la "Passion de l'Inceste": Introduction au Structuralisme*. Paris, 1968.

Steiner, G. *Language and Silence*. New York, 1967.

Thompson, D. A. N. *On Growth and Form*. Cambridge, 1961.

Van Gennep, A. *L'état actuel du problème totémique*. Paris, 1920.

White, L. *The Science of Culture*. New York, 1949.

# INDEX